Who the Hell is Ayn Rand?

Who the hell is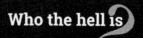

For students, teachers and curious minds, our **carefully structured jargon-free series** helps you really get to grips with brilliant intellectuals and their inherently complex theories.

Written in an **accessible and engaging** way, each book takes you through the **life and influences** of these brilliant intellectuals, before taking a deep dive into three of their **key theories in plain English.**

Smart thinking made easy!

POLITICS   PSYCHOLOGY   PHILOSOPHY   SOCIOLOGY   ART HISTORY

Who the Hell is Friedrich Nietzsche?
"...accessible and unambiguous... clarity and accuracy... highly recommend this book"

Jamie Corish, The Philosophy Foundation

Who the Hell is B.F. Skinner?
"...an outstanding biography of the man and his theories ...a must read"

Professor Sir Cary Cooper, CBE, University of Manchester

Who the Hell is Karl Marx?
"...accessible without losing any depth of analysis"

Judy Cox, *Socialist Review*

Who the Hell is Jean-Jacques Rousseau?
"...this is exactly what I need. Depth of analysis, yet written in an easily digestible style."

Jay, A level Philosophy teacher

Who the Hell is Karl Marx?
"...pulls Marx right out of that 'difficult' box into an accessible summary of his life and ideas."

Solomon Hughes, *Morning Star*

Who the Hell is Ayn Rand?

And what are her theories all about?

Simon Lemieux

First published in Great Britain in 2022 by
Bowden & Brazil Ltd
Felixstowe, Suffolk, UK.

British Library Cataloguing-in-Publication Data
A CIP record for this book is available from The British Library.

ISBN 978-1-915177-03-2

To find out more about other books and authors in this series,
visit www.whothehellis.co.uk

Contents

Introduction

'It's a bird, it's a plane, it's Ayn Rand!'

Afictional quote referencing the American superhero, Superman, might seem a rather unorthodox way to introduce a study about the controversial, libertarian, free-market-capitalism political thinker and novelist, Ayn Rand. Yet, this opening quote makes sense on several counts and, arguably, in an unconventional way it is referenced indirectly in some of her writings. First, just as Superman – or indeed any number of familiar superheroes including Captain America and Batman – epitomizes American culture, so too does Ayn Rand. Her ideas and political thought are deeply embedded in America's self-perception as a land of the free, of rugged individualism, and as embracing unabashed capitalism. Second, it in part reflects the influence of the German philosopher Friedrich Nietzsche (1844–1900) on her ideas. Nietzsche frequently wrote about a higher caste of humankind that he termed the übermensch, which translates as 'superman' or 'superhuman'. We will look at this further in Chapter 2. Beyond doubt though, is how the whole notion of superheroes/superhumans ties in with the centrality of Rand's philosophy of the strong, resourceful and creative individual who rises above the mediocrity around them. Finally, Rand's first jobs in the USA, following her emigration from the Soviet Union, were as a Hollywood screenwriter and film extra: a fitting beginning for a writer whose philosophy is based around the notion of the individual who refuses to be defeated by the mediocrity and villainy all around them.

However, that is where the similarity between Superman and her own 'superheroes' ends. Rand's fictional heroes are freedom-loving, self-sufficient, autonomous individuals driven by reason, not hope, emotion or a sense of duty. They are individuals who value personal achievement and self-worth above everything else. While Rand's emphasis on individual liberty and rights reflects key underlying themes in American politics and culture, not least the Declaration of Independence and the American Constitution, in many ways she represented a break with much else that might be regarded as typical of American society and values. There was no place in Rand's universe for 'One Nation under God'. Hers was a world view without the spiritual, the mystical and the supernatural. Atheism and logic went hand-in-hand for Rand. Nor did she have any time for a manufactured populist patriotism towards the nation state. She advocated a minimalist and strictly limited government, one that largely stayed out of people's lives. For Rand, the state was never part of the solution, but central to the problem.

To pigeonhole Rand as a conventional right-wing conservative, though, would be seriously wide of the mark, as her atheism and liberal views on social issues, including abortion, demonstrate. Yet nor was she a fully-fledged libertarian or reckless libertine. Although she frequently wrote and talked about the 'virtue of selfishness', she never advocated a society where everyone based their actions on brutish urges and fleeting pleasures regardless of the impact of their actions on others. Rand always placed a high value on purpose and self-esteem. Purpose to her meant working to achieve the type of happiness an individual decides to pursue but one that goes hand-in-hand with self-esteem; that is, the sense that an individual is both worthy enough of that happiness and sufficiently self-confident to embrace the belief that the mind and reason alone hold all the answers to life's challenges and decision making.

To study Ayn Rand is to explore a thinker who adopted elements of liberalism and anarchism (especially her emphasis on the ego) yet who remains an icon for many on America's political right. For example, an article in *The Washington Post* on former Republican House Speaker and 2012 vice presidential candidate, Paul Ryan (b.1970), reports:

> *'Ryan has referenced Rand repeatedly over the course of his career, saying her writings got him into economics and policy. […] Ryan [said]: "I think Ayn Rand did the best job of anybody to build a moral case of capitalism, and that morality of capitalism is under assault."'*
> (Weiner, 2012)

However, her ardent admirers are countered by an equally strong band of opponents, with *The Guardian* newspaper columnist Jonathan Freedland (b.1967) describing Rand as the 'poster girl of a particularly hardcore brand of free-market fundamentalism' (Freedland, 2017). Rand is not an easy political thinker to categorize, or indeed easy to remain neutral about.

Any analysis of Rand is also an exploration of a thinker who conveyed her core ideas primarily through her novels rather than through academic articles or works of abstract philosophy. Yet she herself was very insistent on the underlying consistency and method in her ideas. She was widely dismissed in her own lifetime and subsequently by mainstream academic philosophers. Many regard her ideas as badly formulated and based on little formal study of philosophy, also accusing her of having a narcissistic personality promoting a selfish and narrow individualism. Probably the most comprehensive, if uncritical, collection of her ideas can be found in *Objectivism: The Philosophy of Ayn Rand* (1991) by one of her disciples and designated heir, Leonard Piekoff (b.1933). The work is based around lectures he delivered on her philosophy which Rand herself attended and endorsed. Perhaps one of the deeper ironies of her legacy is how her followers splintered into two groups: the Ayn Rand Institute and The Atlas Foundation. The former advocates a much narrower, more orthodox interpretation of her works, while the latter promotes a more open approach to her ideas, a more liberal objectivism that is open to interpretation. The notion of competing claims for her legacy seems an appropriate tribute in many ways for a writer whose worldview very much embraced competition and the free market.

Rand, whatever one's own view about her philosophical ability or the ideas themselves, is undeniably an influential thinker, especially in the USA. She was a public philosopher who sought to make her ideas accessible and relevant, not least via television interviews. Her novels became bestsellers yet received little critical acclaim and many acerbic reviews. Taken from the

Preface to her non-fiction work, *For the New Intellectual* (1961), Rand's personal view was thus:

> '*I am often asked whether I am primarily a novelist or a philosopher. The answer is: both. In a certain sense, every novelist is a philosopher, because one cannot present a picture of human existence without a philosophical framework. [...] In order to define, explain and present my concept of man, I had to become a philosopher in the specific meaning of the term.*'

While it is stating the obvious that all philosophers and political thinkers are products of their own time, culture and lived experiences, for Ayn Rand this is perhaps truer than for most. Any study of her life and career also has to grasp that her life and attitudes became increasingly embittered and intolerant as the years advanced. Rand developed and refined her ideas over time, but in a way that often became more rigid and less open to discussion and genuine debate, even amongst her own followers and devotees.

This short introduction to her life, key ideas and writings will aim for balance and clarity in assessing the work and legacy of this polarizing individual. Beginning with her life story and the key personal, cultural and intellectual influences on her ideas, the focus will then move onto an analysis of her approach to politics, capitalism and morality. Above all, this study will seek to unpack what objectivism – her own philosophy and guide to life – stands for. Finally, the extent and nature of her legacy will be evaluated. Throughout the book, key elements and themes in her novels will be interwoven as examples to highlight her views, as one cannot make sense of Rand without understanding her novels.

Ayn Rand's Timeline

Ayn Rand

1905	Alisa Zinovyevna Rosenbaum is born in St. Petersburg, Soviet Union
1917	Forced to flee St Petersburg
1921	Graduates from high school; Enrols at Petrograd State University
1924	Graduates from university; Enrols at State Institute for Cinematography in Leningrad
1925	Granted American visa
1926	Arrives in Hollywood; Meets Frank
1929	Marries Frank O'Connor
1931	Becomes US citizen
1936	First novel, **We the Living** is published
1938	Novella **Anthem** is published in England
1940	Works on Wendell Willkie's presidential campaign; **The Unconquered** opens and closes within a week on Broadway
1943	**The Fountainhead** is published
1945	Begins work on **Atlas Shrugged**
1947	Testifies at HUAC hearings in Washington DC

World Events

1905	First Russian Revolution begins
1914	WWI breaks out
1917	Bolshevik Revolution begins
1918	Spanish flu and Russian typhus epidemic begins; WWI ends
1920	Women gain the right to vote in the USA
1921	New Economic Policy created by Lenin; famine takes hold in Russia
1922	Fascist leader Mussolini seizes power in Italy
1929	Wall Street Crash; Great Depression begins
1932	Franklin D. Roosevelt is elected President of the United States
1934	Adolf Hitler becomes Chancellor of Germany
1940	Leon Trotsky is assassinated
1945	WWII ends
1947	Cold War between USA and Soviet Union begins

1949	*The Fountainhead* film is released
1951	Moves to New York
	1955 Vietnam War begins
	1956 Suez Crisis; Hungarian Revolution
1957 *Atlas Shrugged* is published	**1957** Sputnik 1 launched into orbit by Soviet Union
1961 *For the New Intellectual* is published	**1961** Bay of Pigs Invasion
1962 First issue of *The Objectivist Newsletter* is published	
1963 Awarded honorary doctorate by Lewis & Clark College	**1963** John F. Kennedy is assassinated
1964 *The Virtue of Selfishness* is published	
1966 *Capitalism: The Unknown Ideal* is published	
	1967 Six-Day War
1968 Breaks off friendship with the Brandens	**1968** Student and worker uprisings in France
	1969 Stonewall riots in New York City
	1975 Vietnam War ends
1976 Undergoes surgery for lung cancer; Writes last article for *The Ayn Rand Letter*	
1979 Frank O'Connor dies	
1982 Ayn Rand dies of heart failure	**1982** Homosexuality is decriminalized in Northern Ireland

1. Rand's Life Story

The eldest of three girls, Ayn Rand was born Alisa Zinovyevna Rosenbaum to a middle-class Jewish-Russian family in St Petersburg, Russia, on 2 February 1905. Alisa's parents were an intriguing pair of individuals. Her father Zinovy Rosenbaum, more commonly known as Fronz, was a quiet, passive man who had earned his degree in chemistry at Warsaw University before setting up his own business as a retail pharmacist in St. Petersburg. Having come from a poor background, he was a self-made man who had succeeded in earning a comfortable middle-class income and, as a result, Alisa and her sisters grew up with a cook, a governess, a nurse and tutors. Her father was one of the Russian Army's favourite tailors and, as a result, the family were protected from much of the anti-Semitism prevalent at that time. Rand's mother, Anna Kaplan, was an educated woman from a cultured and wealthy family. In contrast to Fronz, Anna was more publicly assertive, fond of parties and was a social climber. She urged her daughter to get along with people she didn't like even if it meant presenting something of a false façade to them; something Alisa refused to do.

Alisa's relationship with her parents was not close. Her father was distant and largely kept to himself. Her mother, meanwhile, was prone to bursts of temper, once breaking the leg of Alisa's favourite doll and another time destroying a photo of the Russian revolutionary, Alexander Kerensky (1881–1970) that Alisa cherished. According to Rand's biographer, Jennifer Burns, Anna 'declared openly that she had never wanted children, hated caring for them, and did so only because it was her duty' (Burns, 2011). Unsurprisingly, one of Rand's early followers Barbara Branden would later recall Rand admitting of her mother: 'I disliked her quite a lot. We really didn't get along. She was my exact opposite, and I thought so in childhood and now.' (The Atlas Society).

A Russian Childhood

Growing up in an elite and privileged family, Alisa spent summers at prestigious resorts on the Crimean peninsula and travelled to Austria and Switzerland for long holidays. Despite their Jewish upbringing, Fronz and Anna led predominantly secular lives with the exception of major Jewish holidays such as Passover. They both considered the European culture of the Enlightenment to be more important than the Jewish culture in which they had been raised and encouraged their daughters to learn French and German, emphasizing that 'culture, civilization, anything which is interesting […] is abroad' (Burns, 2011). Having grown up in such a cultured household, it is perhaps not surprising that Rand declared that she had decided to become an author at just nine years old. By 13 she had become a committed atheist and, at the age of 16, she attempted to write her first novel. She also became an avid film fan. In her late teens, Alisa kept a diary in which she recorded every (silent) movie she saw, along with a list of the cast, director, date and a grade rating. As a result, she developed a fascination with America in her early years, even naming the family cats after American cities and states.

An Educated Loner

Alisa received considerable tutoring at home before going to the prestigious Stoiunina Gymnasium where she excelled in lessons but struggled to fit in socially. She thought differently to the other girls in her class, disliked their penchant for gossip and described herself as 'bashful because I literally didn't know what to talk to people about' (Burns, 2011). Her school years were lonely ones. She was never asked out on dates and was never invited to parties. She put her peers' rejection down to jealousy of her intelligence. According to her biographer, 'Alisa was starting to understand herself as a heroine unfairly punished for what was best in her. Later she would come to see envy and resentment as fundamental social and political problems' (Burns, 2011). By way of escape, Alisa lost herself in the stories of princesses and adventurers in the French children's magazines that her mother gave her to improve her French. This led her to begin writing her own stories at school, while pretending to study, reading them to her sisters Nora and Natasha at bedtime.

As the Russian Revolution raged on, the Bolsheviks seized and nationalized Fronz's pharmacy. Refusing to take a job with the communist soviet state, Fronz declared 'I will never work for them! Not now and not ever. Not even if we starve' (The Atlas Society). As a consequence, the family fled to the Crimean peninsula, which was still under czarist rule, and Fronz opened up another shop. Alisa, now a teenager, went to the local school where she was top of her class thanks to her elite city education. But three years later Crimea fell to the Communists and the Rosenbaums once again had their business confiscated. Returning to St Petersburg, which had been renamed Petrograd, they ended up living in a few rooms in the apartment building they had once owned. The year 1921–22 was when the Russian famine hit, resulting in five million Russians starving to death. It was a very bleak time for the Rosenbaums who existed on a diet of millet, acorns and mush. Rand recalled to friends later in her life how 'she wrapped newspapers around her feet in lieu of shoes' and 'how she had begged her mother for a last dried pea to stave off her hunger' (Burns, 2011).

Ironically, under czarist rule, most opportunities for higher education were closed to women, a situation that only changed with the advent of communist rule when the Bolsheviks liberalized admission policies, making tuition free. Alisa was therefore able to enrol at Petrograd State University (now St Petersburg). Despite their dire situation, the Rosenbaums somehow managed to scrape together enough money to make sure Alisa could travel to and from university.

Intellectual Development

It was at this time that Alisa finally found a connection with her father. Having been secretly keeping abreast of the political situation, despite being forbidden to do so, one day Alisa asked Fronz if she could accompany him to a political meeting that he was attending. Surprised by her request, he agreed and the two became political allies, forging a long-missing connection. Both were anti-Communist, or 'pro-individualist' as Rand would later describe it, which safeguarded her against being radicalized at the university. The Bolsheviks had made sure that any counterrevolutionary professors were either dismissed or intimidated and they introduced Marxist courses on historical materialism and political economy instead.

Anti-Communist students and professors, including Alisa, were incensed and protested against the forced conformity. But the Bolsheviks responded with purges and many agitators disappeared. Alisa grew quieter in her dissent after that and spent her three years at the university avoiding the larger lectures which favoured Communist ideology, instead choosing the smaller seminars. Unsurprisingly, much of Alisa's education at university was Marxist leaning, but she also studied history, the history of worldviews, psychology, French, biology, logic, and philosophy. It was this last subject that shaped her intellectual outlook, encountering as she did the work of Plato (c.427–347 BC), Aristotle (384–322 BC), Nietzsche and Friedrich Hegel (1770–1831). The full impact of her exposure to Russian philosophy will be discussed further in Chapter 2.

Goodbye to Russia

The revolutionary upheavals and subsequent brutality that Alisa witnessed throughout her educational years made her determined to escape a totalitarian regime which seemed to close down all opportunities for individualism, free thought and self-advancement. In October 1924, she graduated in history from what was by that time now called the University of Leningrad. Having decided to embark on a career in screenwriting, she enrolled at the State Institute for Cinematography in Leningrad. It was while still in Russia that her first published work appeared: a monograph on

Fig. 1 Cover of Rand's first book, *Pola Negri*, published in 1925 in Moscow, Russia.

the Polish actress Pola Negri (1897–1987) who, in 1922, had become the first European actress to be contracted to a Hollywood studio. Published by Moscow & Leningrad in 1925 under the name of A. Rosenbaum, the monograph was part of a series on movie stars and it represents the first tangible evidence of Rand's attraction to the USA, and especially to its creative and artistic side.

In 1925, after much work, not least by her mother who had to investigate all the rules and regulations regarding foreign travel, Alisa managed to get both a passport and a visa to visit relatives in the United States. She left her country of birth at the beginning of 1926, never to return.

Moving to America

Upon arriving in America, Alisa Zinovyevna Rosenbaum became Ayn Rand; 'Rand' being an abbreviation of her Russian surname, (Heller, 2009) and Ayn, from the Finnish name Aino (Ayn Rand Archives). The end result certainly sounded pithier. She spent six months with relatives in Chicago, one of whom owned a cinema which enabled her to watch dozens of films. She then left for Hollywood where she had a lucky encounter with the film director and producer, Cecil B. DeMille (1881–1959) on her second day. This led to a job as an extra on his film *The King of Kings* (1927), a film biopic about Jesus – somewhat ironic given Rand's atheism. She then secured roles as a script reader and, later, as a junior screenwriter.

Falling in Love

It was during her time in Hollywood that she met the actor Frank O'Connor (1897–1979) who had caught her eye when they were both working on the set of *The King of Kings*. They were married in 1929 and remained together until his death in 1979. O'Connor later worked as a flower grower when they lived on a ranch in California, then as an artist when they moved to New York. The marriage was largely successful albeit somewhat unconventional in certain respects, with aspects of the 'open marriage' covered later in this chapter.

O'Connor is one of the many paradoxes in Rand's life. For someone who valued the intellect so highly, Frank might appear a slightly strange choice of partner for Rand. He was neither a ruthless and highly successful industrialist, nor did he achieve great renown or reward with his acting or art. Instead, the attraction for Rand was mostly physical. As she herself commented, 'I took one look at him and, you know, Frank is the physical type of all my heroes. I instantly fell in love' (Grossman, 2016). Contemporaries who knew the couple commented that O'Connor never publicly disagreed with his wife over politics or philosophy, nor did he hold particularly distinctive ideas of his own. Where she recognized his physical attributes above all else, he recognized her undoubted intelligence and charisma, and appears to have been largely content to play the part of loyal consort.

Some of Rand's biographers have noted how, when Rand wanted sex, Frank would sometimes be summoned into the house when he was out tending the flowers on the ranch. Although Rand idolized the dominant-heroic type in her books, in her own life it was she who was the dominant one in her relationship. In his later years, Frank became housebound and suffered from dementia, something Rand found especially hard to accept. She was grief-stricken when he died.

Finding a Career

Rand became an American resident in 1929, and a citizen in 1931. She was the breadwinner right from the beginning of her marriage and held down various jobs during the 1930s to support her writing, working for a time as head of the costume department at RKO Radio Pictures in Hollywood. It was during this time that her first efforts at commercial writing appeared and

Fig. 2 Front of flyer advertising the Broadway production of *Night of January 16th*, 1935.

she sold her first screenplay *Red Pawn* in 1932 to Universal Studios, although it was never produced. She also wrote a court-room drama *Night of January 16th*, a play that opened as *Woman on Trial* at the Hollywood Playhouse in 1934, before transferring to Broadway for a moderately successful season in 1934–5. It was published in hardcover much later in 1968. Her first published novel, *We the Living*, which was set in revolutionary Russia and was semi-autobiographical, was written in 1934 though not released until 1936 as it was rejected by several publishers. A stage version of the book opened briefly on Broadway in 1940 as *The Unconquered* but, despite her high hopes, it was both a critical and financial failure and closed within a week.

Rand experienced a great deal of rejection and setbacks to her writing career in the 1930s. In addition, she also made several attempts during this time to bring her parents and sisters to the United States, but they were unable to acquire permission to emigrate. Sadly, both Anna and Fronz would die without seeing their eldest daughter again.

Arriving alone and virtually penniless in the USA, and having to rely on initiative, persistence and her own inner-resolve, may in part explain her philosophy, focused as it was around self-determination and resourcefulness. What she perhaps forgot, or was far less willing to admit in her political ideas, was the help and support she received from others, including friends and family, in her quest for fame and acclaim.

A Degree of Success

Literary success and a degree of fortune would have to wait till the next decade when, after some initial reluctance from the publishing industry, *The Fountainhead* was published in 1943. Again, publication was not straightforward; it was rejected by many publishers before finally being accepted by Bobbs-Merrill and went on to sell in excess of six and a half million copies with a film adaptation following in 1949. The unexpected success of the novel propelled Rand into the limelight and led to her meeting with prominent West Coast conservatives. Like her, they feared a growing and insidious communist influence at work in the land of the free. In 1947, Rand herself testified at the House Un-American Activities Committee (HUAC) as part of their investigations into supposed left-wing influence in Hollywood.

Her most iconic, lengthy and final fictional work *Atlas Shrugged* would appear in 1957, having taken some 10 years to write and, to date, has sold well over seven million copies. Rand had little trouble securing a publisher for *Atlas Shrugged*, though she rejected Bobbs-Merrill when they wanted to discuss cuts and edits. Instead, it would be published by Random House. A film trilogy based on the novel appeared between 2011–2014, though failed to recoup the costs of making the films. Both *The Fountainhead* and *Atlas Shrugged* are central to understanding Rand's ideas and will figure prominently in the key theory chapters. Suffice to say that both focus on strong-willed, creative, capitalist characters fighting against an overbearing state and individuals who favour consensus and lack ideas of their own; 'takers' not 'makers', as Rand would have it.

From this point on, Rand focused on non-fiction, giving talks and lectures and writing for *The Objectivist Newsletter*. She produced several shorter tracts such as *For the New Intellectual* in 1961, which contained excerpts from many of the key speeches given by her fictional heroes in her novels, and *The Virtue of Selfishness* in 1964, where she focused on the rejection of altruism and living one's life for others – a theme also covered later on in this book.

The Collective and Objectivism

Throughout this time Rand and O'Connor were living in New York, having moved there from California in 1951. Rand was an active presence on the intellectual New York scene and sought out 'reactionaries' as friends. She became a magnet for libertarians and before long had amassed a small group of followers ironically calling themselves 'The Collective'; ironic because, alongside altruism, collectivism was one of the values most rejected by Rand and her circle. Among the group was the economist Alan Greenspan (b.1926), who later went on to serve as chairman of the US Federal Reserve Bank. It was Rand who influenced Greenspan to broaden his approach to economics, which had previously been strictly empirical: 'Rand persuaded [him] to look at human beings, their values, how they work, what they do and why they do it, and how they think and why they think.' (Greenspan, 2007).

Her leadership of The Collective, comprising almost entirely of younger devotees, was ironically increasingly autocratic. While her whole philosophy was based around individualism, in reality agreement with Rand was a necessity to remain a member of the group. The economist and self-styled anarcho-capitalist, Murray Rothbard (1926–95), who loosely associated with the group for a while, commented that the famous individualist actually denied individuality among her closest followers. Rand presided over this inner circle of objectivism's 'true believers' in a manner partly resembling that of a society hostess dispensing favours and introductions, and partly resembling a religious guru, imparting deep insights and delivering the final verdict in all matters of truth. We will look at Rand's Objectivist philosophy in Chapter 3.

A Dark Side

A less attractive side to Rand's personality was the tendency to break off friendships and relationships with those who either disagreed or questioned aspects of her definition of objectivism, or she fell out with them for other reasons. One example is the psychotherapist and writer, Nathaniel Branden (1930–2014) who, along with his first wife Barbara Weidman (1929–2013), was an early disciple of Rand and part of The Collective.

In the 1950s, Rand had an affair with Branden and, in true Rand style, the decision to embark on such a coupling was formally explained to their respective partners. Indeed, an arrangement was made that Rand and Branden would have twice-weekly dates for sex in her apartment, with Frank expected to discreetly take leave of his wife for the duration of the lovers' tryst. Rand and the 25-years younger Branden viewed the arrangement as a natural step for 'higher-rational' people who valued openness, honesty and owning up to one's deeper desires above all else. Such was the philosophical closeness between Rand and Branden that, in 1958 with Rand's support, Branden created the Nathaniel Branden Lectures, later renamed the Nathaniel Branden Institute (NBI). This organization spread objectivism by offering live and taped lecture courses by a variety of Objectivist intellectuals, including Rand, Branden himself, and Alan Greenspan. Branden's work at the NBI included putting together the principles, expressed by Rand in her fiction and non-fiction writing, into a more systematized structure – a kind of Objectivist manual.

However, when in 1964 Nathaniel Branden began an affair with the young actress Patrecia Scott (1940–1977), who he later married, both Nathaniel and Barbara kept the affair hidden from

Rand for fear of her reaction, even though the affair between Rand and Branden had ended somewhile back. When she did come to learn of it in 1968, their fears proved correct. Rand abruptly terminated her relationship with both Brandens which in turn led to the closure of the NBI. In September 1968, Rand published a damning and highly personalized attack in *The Objectivist*, stating,

Fig. 3 Portrait of Rand used for the back cover of *Atlas Shrugged*, 1957.

> '*I hereby withdraw my endorsement of them [the Brandens] and of their future works and activities [...] I repudiate both of them, totally and permanently, as spokesmen for me or for Objectivism. At my lowest opinion of Mr. Branden's behavior, I had not expected conscious deception on his part. I have always been willing to give a person the benefit of the doubt in regard to errors of knowledge—and I had extended that benefit for too long in the case of Mr. Branden. I have never accepted, condoned or tolerated conscious breaches of morality. This was the last of the evidence which caused me to break all professional, as well as personal, association with him.*'

It would seem that anyone who disagreed with Rand's interpretation of objectivism was regarded by her as wrong, misguided and irrational. To embrace individualism within objectivism was, then, to embrace what Rand said about individualism. One of Branden's 'crimes', which he subsequently set out in his 1984 response to Rand's excoriation of him and his wife, was to argue that while there was much to admire in her writing and work, she could also be prone to a refusal to engage constructively with any critics. He says,

> *'She could be abrasive; she could make sweeping generalizations that needed explanations that she did not provide; she made very little effort to understand someone else's intellectual context and to build a bridge from their context to hers [...] Of all the accusations of her critics, surely the most ludicrous is the accusation that Ayn Rand encourages people to do just what they please. If there's anything in this world Ayn did not do, it was to encourage people to do what they please. If there is anything she was not, it was an advocate of hedonism [...]; on the one hand she preached a morality of joy, personal happiness, and individual fulfilment; on the other hand, she was a master at scaring the hell out of you if you respected and admired her and wanted to apply her philosophy to your own life.'* (Branden, 1984)

It is worth reflecting at some length on this falling out between Rand and Branden for what it suggests about aspects of her personality. Clearly, there was something very charismatic about her and the ideas she advocated; enough to draw in devoted admirers. At one level, her ideas about self-interest, personal freedom and self-ownership struck a chord with many, especially young idealists such as the Brandens. Yet there was a rigidity and certainty about her approach; those who were not with her 110%, were against her. Missing from her writing, both fiction and non-fiction, appears to be much real sense of empathy or understanding with those who took a different stance to her. Just as with her literary works, she had little time for those who sought with the best of motives to edit or re-work her ideas. Another example is her agent, Ann Watkins, who had done much to help her in her early days as a writer and with who Rand parted on bad terms. Rand was uncompromising, which to her fans was part of the allure, part of her self-esteem and inner fortitude, but which for others made her a difficult person to work with. In *The New Criterion*, Anthony Daniels writes,

> *'Though she could be charming, it was not something she could keep up for long. She was deeply ungrateful to those who had helped her and many of her friendships ended in acrimony. Her biographer tells us that she sometimes told jokes, but, in the absence of any supportive evidence, I treat reports of her sense of humour much as I treat reports of sightings of the Loch Ness Monster: apocryphal at best.'* (Daniels, 2010)

An Unconventional Philosopher

Rand never followed the conventional route of most 20th- and 21st-century philosophers, such as her American contemporaries Robert Nozick (1938–2002) and John Rawls (1921–2002), namely holding down positions in university philosophy departments, pursuing doctorate level research and publishing academic papers. But in many ways this is not that surprising. Not only did Rand have little interest in formal academic recognition, but she also lacked any great ambition for academic research and collaborative learning and study. For her, proper philosophy – by which she meant objectivism – was an instructional guide to living in the present, not learning for its own sake. Hence, her energies were spent on spreading the word and publicizing her views through writing and lecturing, often in the face of indifferent or critical academics, although she did receive an honorary doctorate from Lewis & Clark University in 1963. Nor, despite her own strong political views, not least about the role of the state and concerning capitalism, did she ever seek elected office or become a prominent political campaigner. Instead, she preferred the medium of her novels and the Objectivist movement that emerged out of them. The only conventional active political campaigning she undertook was helping with the unsuccessful 1940 campaign of Republican Wendell Willkie (1892–1944), who lost to incumbent president Franklin D. Roosevelt (1882–1945). Rand was motivated in large part by her strong opposition to Roosevelt's New Deal, which in her mind smacked of collectivism and threatened to destroy the 'rugged individualism' which she so admired in the USA. Self-help, she feared, would be replaced by unearned entitlement. Essentially, Rand remained devoted to and dominated by her writing, saying, 'I have no hobbies. Nothing besides writing ever mattered to me too much' (Heller, 2009).

For much of the latter part of her life, Rand continued to give public lectures and talks, as well as writing pieces for her assorted journals. In the early 1960s, she gave numerous lectures and also Q and A sessions at leading American universities including Yale, Princeton and MIT. Her lectures were usually full, and she enjoyed promoting her beliefs to a youthful and often appreciative audience. She could certainly be a compelling public speaker. Starting in 1961 she delivered a lecture annually for the next 18 years at a famous bastion of free speech, the Ford Hall Forum at Northeastern University in Boston. She was regarded as a maverick but exciting and stimulating speaker who never lost her thick Russian accent, which perhaps added to her mystique. Considering she was active at the height of the Cold War (c.1947–91), when Russia was identified as Uncle Sam's main enemy, Rand's perseverance and success was quite extraordinary, with many of the initially sceptical going on to buy her books and move closer to her belief system. She gave her final public lecture in November 1981 in New Orleans just months before her death.

Final Years and Beyond

A heavy smoker, Rand had surgery for lung cancer in 1974 and died from heart failure in 1982. She had no children and no heir, as her husband Frank had died three years earlier. The guardian of her legacy was Leonard Peikoff, a Canadian-born philosophy teacher who was instrumental in founding the Ayn Rand Institute. At the time of her death, Rand was working on the script for a television adaptation of *Atlas Shrugged*. Appropriately, given the final sentence in *Atlas Shrugged* where her hero, John Galt, traces a dollar sign in the air, one of the floral tributes at her funeral was in the shape of a dollar sign. She was buried alongside her husband at Kensico Cemetery in Valhalla, New York.

Fig. 4 Gravestones of Ayn Rand and her husband Frank O'Connor, Kensico Cemetery in Valhalla, New York.

Regardless of how some of her critics viewed her (including those on the political right), Rand maintains a loyal and devoted following. Several collections of previously unpublished works and letters have appeared since her death. For those who seek an alternative libertarian revolution and utopia, she retains the status of a secular deity. She represents a uniquely inspired guru, one of the few novelists and essayists to criticize and critique contemporary society. To her critics, she represents a second-rate writer, whose pseudo-philosophy elevated the strong, despised the weak and sowed dangerous ideas into young minds. Her life and career straddled the influences of both czarist and communist Russia, Hollywood, and the revolutionary interpretation of liberty US-style. It is those varied and often contradictory influences which we will turn to now.

2. Influences on Rand's Thinking

While Rand publicly acknowledged a debt to the French novelist Victor Hugo (1802–85), the Greek philosopher Aristotle and the Catholic theologian, Thomas Aquinas (1225–1274), the basic tenets of objectivism – reality, reason, self-interest and capitalism – she claimed to be her own creation. In reality – a word much beloved of Rand – there was rather more to it. Rand, like all thinkers and philosophers, was very much a product of her time as well as of her education and personal experiences. Not only did her life, both in Russia and in America, impact on her thinking but there were many philosophers, writers and people she met along the way that would influence the direction in which Rand's life went.

A Russian Thinker

It is too easy to simply dismiss Rand's time in Russia as leading her to conclude that she did not endorse Communism, statism and – from the czarist era – Christian mysticism. In actual fact, this time of her life had a profound impact on her future ideas and intellectual development and, while she rejected Russian politics and philosophy, she remained a very Russian thinker.

This is evident in her passion, in her sweeping generalizations, in her determination to turn her ideals into a practical reality. Like many Russian thinkers before her, she was a non-academic philosopher who rejected dualism in favour of a unified system, where everything relates to everything else. Dualism in philosophy is the belief that everything comprises diametrically opposed positions, such as theory and practice; idealism and materialism; reason and emotion; rationalism and empiricism. Such views can never ultimately be reconciled to one another but exist in tension as polar opposites.

In Russia, however, philosophy is never just a theoretical practice, but a social commitment. According to one of the leading scholars on Rand, Chris Sciabarra, Rand's philosophy 'is as much defined by what she accepted in Russian thought as by what she rejected'. He goes on to argue that her intellectual development 'reflects the very Hegelian Aufhebung she ridiculed as a violation of the law of identity. [She] both absorbed and abolished, preserved and transcended, the elements of her Russian past' (Sciabarra, 1995). What Sciabarra is referring to is Hegel's theory of dialectics whereby everything relates to each other and is part of a single over-arching system. Ideas begin with a proposition (thesis) and a counter-proposition (antithesis), and eventually a combination of ideas (or synthesis) emerges through the process of reason and rigorous intellectual debate and dialogue. Rand enthusiastically embraced this approach in her own philosophical thought, often synthesizing two opposing points of view to form a single unified approach (see A Marxian Approach below).

A Russian Education

It was during her time at university that Rand would have read the bulk of her philosophy in the formal academic manner. These were crucial years in her intellectual formation. Although it could hardly be said to have been a high-quality education with propaganda rife in course material, Rand did recognize that, under the Soviets, she had learnt a method of 'thinking in principles' and of maintaining a critical outlook. She said, 'No matter what you are taught, listen to it critically, whether you agree or not. And if you disagree, formulate your reasons [...] Under the Soviets [...] I learned a great deal, but only in that way' (Rand quoted in Sciabarra, 1995).

The professor at Petrograd University who had the most important influence on Rand was her philosophy professor, Nikolay Lossky (1870–1965). Lossky's philosophy was a combination of idealism and realism: he put forward an 'ideal-realist' approach that pursued a 'unity of opposites' (Lossky, 1951). While he shared many of the beliefs of Platonists, Lossky argued that his ideal-realist approach was based on Aristotle's thinking:

> *'According to Aristotle, every particular thing and being in the world is the result of the combination of matter and form [...] Abstraction being made of these definite characteristics of concrete things, matter is conceived of as the possibility of any one of these forms or characteristics.'*
> (Lossky, [1917] 1928)

Lossky would almost certainly have introduced Rand to Hegel's dialectical method and, without a doubt, taught her the ideas of the Greek philosophers, Plato and Aristotle. She would also have come into contact with Nietzsche, whose voice can be heard from time to time in Rand's work.

Dionysian Symbolism and a 'Will to Power'

While, essentially, Rand openly rejected much of Nietzsche's philosophy, with the exception of his critique on altruism and Christianity, she did have a philosophical interest in his work. This manifested from the historical context within which Rand lived during her formative years: the Silver Age. After the Russian Revolution, there was an explosion of creative activity in the literary arts when philosophers, writers, poets and artists rejected positivism and materialism and began exploring freedom, truth and beauty. One artistic movement in particular – Russian Symbolism – embraced the philosophy of Nietzsche, in particular the Dionysian aspects where he theorizes that all great art arises from the meeting of two opposites. The symbolism Nietzsche used has its origins in Greek tragedy, whereby the Dionysian (relating to Dionysus, the Greek god of wine and music) represents the dark foolish power of the subconscious, while the Apollonian (relating to Apollo, the Greek god of light and art) represents the rational methodical conscious mind.

While Rand rejected the way that Nietzsche viewed reason and emotion separately, she did see purpose in the symbolism that he had used. Looking at the two major events of the summer of 1969, the Apollo 11 moon landing and the Woodstock music festival, Rand explored the philosophical meaning and causes of these two events in her 1969 lecture 'Apollo and Dionysus' at Boston's Ford Hall Forum. She applied Nietzsche's Apollonian–Dionysian symbolism in her examination of reason versus irrational emotion which she saw as 'the fundamental conflict of our age' (Rand, 1971).

In *The Fountainhead*, we again see Nietzsche's influence on Rand's thinking. The antagonist in the novel, Ellsworth Toohey, is portrayed as a parody of Nietzsche's concept of 'the will to power' (a powerful natural life force that we can use to push ourselves into becoming superhuman). Rand describes her character as having 'an insane will to power, a lust for superiority that can be expressed only through others', that ultimately inverts and obliterates all values (Sciabarra, 1995). At the same time, Rand uses Toohey to casually honour Nietzsche by making the philosopher Toohey's scapegoat. Referring to Nietzsche, Toohey remarks 'It is not our function—paraphrasing a philosopher whom we do not like—to be a fly swatter, but when a fly acquires delusions of grandeur, the best of us must stoop to do a little job of extermination' (Rand, 1943). Toohey again refers to Nietzsche when mocking the protagonist of the novel, Howard Roark, by adding a caption saying 'Are you happy, Mr Superman?' below a photograph of Roark in his newspaper (1943).

According to Sciabarra, Toohey also symbolizes the essence of the Russian sobernost – the spiritual community of a united people – which Rand was so against. Sciabarra explains:

> *'Toohey's newspaper column, "One Small Voice," features endless attacks against individualism that reek of Russian sobornost. In many ways, he extols the virtue of the cultic loss of self, a theme that was prominent in the writings of the Nietzschean Russian Symbolists.'*
> (Sciabarra, 1995)

Later, Rand's Objectivist philosophy would take Nietzsche's 'will to power' and create a 'will to efficacy', which expounds the belief that we have the power to turn our thoughts and desires into successful actions, enabling us to have cognitive control over our lives.

Aristotle's Rationalism and Empiricism

A philosopher Rand openly admitted to being a big influence on her intellectual and philosophical development, was Aristotle. His emphasis on rationalism and empiricism is evident in Rand's own philosophy of objectivism. Rand's ideas focus on both metaphysics, namely the study of the nature of the universe as a whole, and epistemology, the study of the theory of knowledge, or 'why and how we know what we know'. Like Aristotle, Rand rejected those elements of Platonic thought that were abstract and utopian. For Plato, things or indeed emotions and actions correspond to an abstract ideal that exists completely outside space and time. The role of the human philosopher, says Plato, is to discover the ultimate 'true' reality through reason. But for Aristotle, knowledge can only be gained by experience – by observing the world around us. He did not see the human condition as a trap distracting the mind from truth, as Plato did, instead he believed that we can use our body as a tool to aid us in extending our learning.

Rand frequently acknowledged Aristotle in her philosophical writings. For example, she was strongly taken by his emphasis on the use of reason, logic and observation to draw conclusions. She praised his emphasis on the individual, arguing that his unparalleled achievement lay in the fact that he defined the basic principles of a rational view of existence and of man's consciousness. Indeed, she called him 'a philosophical Atlas who carries the whole of Western civilization on his shoulders' (cited in Daniels, 2010). A further acknowledged debt to Aristotle is in the titles that Rand gave to the three parts of her novel *Atlas Shrugged* (Non-Contradiction, Either-Or, A is A) and to one of the chapters (The Immovable Movers). Rand even makes the grandiose assertion that:

> *'If we consider the fact that to this day everything that makes us civilized beings, every rational value that we possess—including the birth of science, the industrial revolution, the creation of the United States, even the structure of our language—is the result of Aristotle's influence, of the degree to which, explicitly or implicitly, men accepted his epistemological principles, we would have to say: never have so many owed so much to one man.'* (Rand, 1963)

This is certainly a claim of some magnitude, and also one open to dispute. To see Aristotle alone as the 'sole genius philosopher' is to ignore Aristotle's own debt to his teacher Plato, and indeed Plato's teacher Socrates. Were there really no civilized people (and logicians) before Aristotle? There is also very little direct quotation of Aristotle in Rand's own essays, indeed the only time Rand has ever quoted Aristotle directly in her writings is in her essay 'Basic Principles of Literature' (1969).

As the academic George H. Smith notes in 'Ayn Rand on Aristotle' (Smith, 2016), it is historically inaccurate to view Aristotle as the father and defender of individual rights; his description of the role of the ideal state was rather more collectivist and welfarist in its own way than Rand acknowledged. Aristotle would certainly have been no defender of the extremely limited state that Rand would advocate. Perhaps, though, Rand was more indirectly influenced by Aristotle's views on slavery and how certain people are 'slaves by nature'. It is important to appreciate that Rand had no sympathy at all for the institution of slavery, even a romanticized one, and strongly denounced racism (see Chapter 5). But where there is a tentative link, perhaps, is in her strict dichotomy between 'creators' and 'looters'; those who strive and think for themselves, and those who – to use her own terms – drift or evade. In that sense, and in that sense only, some of humanity choose to enslave their own minds by their lack of applying reason and logic. They represent those who blindly follow, as opposed to the 'true heroes' who strive and create.

The Logic of Thomas Aquinas

Thomas Aquinas was a philosopher and theologian from the 13th century. In many ways, Rand's public acknowledgement of his significance and relevance to her thinking is highly surprising because, as already discussed, Rand rejected all forms of formal and organized religion. So where does he fit into her philosophical influences? The answer is that, although she would disagree with the spiritual dimension of his thinking, much as she did with Lossky, she admired the huge value he placed on logic, his application of Aristotelian reason, and his creation of a truly systematic understanding of Christian theology.

We can see Aquinas' (and hence Aristotle's) influence on Rand by way of her understanding of 'consciousness'. She saw consciousness as both a faculty of awareness and a state of awareness – something fundamental to all living beings: the ego, the self, the I. As Sciabarra, explains: For Rand,

> '*Consciousness involves three distinct and interactive levels of awareness: sensation, perception, and conception. Each of these levels is a relation between consciousness and existence. There is no such thing as a disembodied mind. Every aspect and process of consciousness has a physical, material component. Rand continues in the grand tradition of Aristotle and Aquinas; she argues that consciousness operates under conditions of materiality and sensuous corporeality.*' (Sciabarra, 1995)

What Sciabarra is saying here is that it is not necessary for thought to be related to things, because it *is* the relation. It is the intelligible way that we make contact with the world, rather than something that we can perceive literally and then relate to things.

A Marxian Approach

Although Rand would have strenuously denied any link between her thinking and that of Karl Marx, there are parallels between their philosophical theories. The obvious link is in their dialectical approach. Marxian 'dialectical materialism' is based on the idea of reflection. Marx believed that our human consciousness is an active reflection of the society that we live in; that the objective material world moulds the structure and content of our consciousness. Therefore, any study of social theory must involve analysis of the whole and avoid taking any part of that whole to be studied separately as a supposed whole in itself. As touched upon earlier in the chapter, Rand's own dialectical method includes her practice of combining two opposing points of view. She recognized the importance of totality, of the intrinsic relationship between dichotomies such as reason and emotion, theory and practice, fact and value. For Rand, these dichotomies are two features of the same organic unity which can only be understood in relation to one another.

Another connection between Marx and Rand's thinking is in their belief that existence comes before essence. In his *Economic and Philosophic Manuscripts of 1844*, Marx writes:

> *'The way in which consciousness is, and in which something is for it, is knowing. Knowing is its sole act. Something therefore comes to be for consciousness insofar as the latter knows this something. Knowing is its sole objective relation.'* (Marx, 1959)

What both Marx and Rand agreed on was that identity or value must be created by the individual alone. Human consciousness and willpower creates its own values; there are no pre-existing values and meanings to be somehow discovered and revealed. The same philosophical construct of existence preceding essence is also found in the writings of the existentialist French philosopher, Jean-Paul Sartre (1905–1980). What Rand would imbibe from her academic studies, both Marxist and non-Marxist, was a belief in a materialist dialecticism. This philosophical term essentially means that ideas only arise from observable material conditions. She would, however, reach a completely different conclusion to

Marx regarding the state and the economy. Her worldview was one that positively endorsed capitalism and individualism over the statism and communalism championed by Marx.

The Russian Effect on Rand's Politics

Rand's childhood experiences of revolutionary Russia, and the subsequent creation of the totalitarian dictatorship of the Soviet Union, fuelled her hatred of socialism and the big state in general. While Marx and his acolytes preached a message of equality, brotherhood and class struggle, Rand rejected these in their entirety. For her, the large, centralised state, whether labelled communist or liberal democratic, inevitably erodes and stifles human freedom and creativity. It is a zero-sum game; the more power the state has, the less autonomy remains with the individual. Rand also reacted strongly against the notion of equality. She believed that inequality is fundamental to human existence and her writing is peppered with superior versus inferior minds, winners and losers, strivers and scroungers. Whereas socialism and communism, and more progressive forms of liberalism, advocate the inalienable rights of individuals to such essentials as food, shelter and medical care, Rand would argue that 'no one owes you a living', least of all the state. You simply deserve what you create and possess. Absent from her worldview is the notion of enforced solidarity with others or class consciousness. As her fictional heroine in *The Fountainhead*, Dominique Francon, puts it, 'To say "I love you", one must first know how to say "I"'. Rand's was a belief system that was in stark contrast to both Soviet totalitarianism, which she had personally witnessed, and the creeping growth of welfarism seen in many

Western democracies, especially after 1945. Rand would no doubt have viewed the British NHS (National Health Service) as nothing less than 'socialized medicine'.

American Politics and Culture

When considering Rand's political philosophy, it is important to do so in the specific American context in which she was writing. All of Rand's major works – both fiction and non-fiction – are written against the backdrop of the Cold War and the attendant 'red scare' (the widespread fear of communism). She began writing her first novel, at least in part, as a response to events in the USA at the time. This was a period very much influenced by Roosevelt, the Democratic president from 1933–1945, and his New Deal. The New Deal represented a huge and unprecedented expansion of central government as a response to the Great Depression of the 1930s. Numerous government agencies were established, pumping in public money to stimulate the economy and to stave off the worst social effects such as mass unemployment. While warmly welcomed by the majority of Americans (Roosevelt was re-elected with ease on three occasions) Rand was alarmed by this growth of statism. For her,

Fig. 5 Poster for the 1935 WPA, an American New Deal agency employing millions of jobseekers for public works projects.

along with those on the political right, there was a real danger that the USA might sleepwalk into soviet-style authoritarianism. Elements of the New Deal, including some of the measures it created, can be seen parodied in *Atlas Shrugged*. One example is the 'Anti Dog-Eat-Dog Act' that aimed to restrict cut-throat competition between businesses and thus reduce the number of business bankruptcies.

Rand fully intended her works to be a rallying cry for supporters of limited government, standing against both the moral and material dangers of the all-powerful state. Less easy for traditional American conservatives to accept were her more libertarian ideas on personal morality, her militant atheism and a criticism of simplistic nationalism. Yet, while she loathed socialism, she embraced a particular view of American culture, above all that famous sentence in the Declaration of Independence:

> *'We hold these truths to be self-evident, that all men are created equal, that they are endowed by their Creator with certain unalienable Rights, that among these are Life, Liberty and the pursuit of Happiness.'*

However, along with the reference to a 'Creator', she was rather less keen on the phrase that followed:

> *'That to secure these rights, Governments are instituted among Men, deriving their just powers from the consent of the governed.'*

The idea of some higher force having created human rights, and a Government being in charge of those rights, did not sit well for Rand. She believed that life, liberty and the pursuit of happiness were an inalienable birth right that protected the individual against the state. For Rand, America at its best represented a 'land of the free' where individuals are able to pursue their own dreams and aspirations – the most noble calling of all. The impact of this emphasis upon individual endeavour and self-sufficiency moulded and shaped much of her thinking, something that is apparent in both her literary heroes and her wider body of thought. So, both implicitly and explicitly, the American Dream concept influenced what she wanted to preserve and reinforce against the tide of welfarism, faith-imposed moralising and greater state intervention. In these two ways, Rand was very much both a product and an influencer of post-war America and its fears and dreams.

Individualists and Free-market Thinkers

During the 1930s and 40s, in particular, Rand was influenced by her relationships with a range of individualist and free-market thinkers. Above all, her views on capitalism were crystallised by encountering the works of individuals such as Ludwig von Mises (1881–1973), the 'father of the modern Austrian school of economics' (Sciabarra, 1995) who taught several influential economic thinkers such as Murray Rothbard and Friedrich Hayek (1899–1992). From von Mises, whose works she cited in her own lectures and writings, she gleaned many of her ideas, including on the superiority of the free market. Where she went further was in searching for (and from her perspective, finding) a moral base and defence for capitalism and the free market, as opposed to a purely economic justification. Again, this reinforces her desire to create a systemic and all-encompassing world view. Free-market capitalism was to be defended not just because it was economically efficient, but because it was morally superior, she claimed. Any dualism of the economic and the moral had no place in Rand's system of thought.

Another of her intellectual influences in America was the libertarian writer and critic, Isabel Paterson (1886–1961). Paterson was an opponent of FDR's New Deal during the 1930s and a strong advocate of individualism and private business. Like Rand, she could write lucidly if sometimes acerbically. She is widely credited for deepening Rand's knowledge of American history and government, as well as introducing her to many key individualist works and thinkers in history, philosophy and economics. For a while, until their estrangement in 1948, they eagerly promoted each other's works. Rand went so far as to describe Paterson's best-known work, *The God of the Machine* (1943) in a letter from that year in superlative terms,

> *"The God of the Machine" is the greatest book written in the last three hundred years. It is the first complete statement of the philosophy of individualism as a political and economic system. It is the basic document of capitalism [...] That is why the American system, which gave mankind the greatest, unprecedented, miraculous blessings, is now in the process of destroying itself. Men do not know what they had, what they are losing and how they are losing it. They had no book to tell them. "The God of the Machine" does for capitalism what the Bible did for Christianity—and, forgive the comparison, what "Das Kapital" did for Communism or "Mein Kampf" for Nazism. It takes a book to save or destroy the world.'* (Ayn Rand archives)

This letter is revealing not only for its uncharacteristic praise of another author, but also for the emphasis on an underlying principle as the basis for all thought, and the call to action to protect what she terms the 'American system'. It also reflects Rand's emphasis on the importance of books and writing in spreading ideas.

1960s America

But how did Rand fit into the wider cultural context of 1960s America? In some ways, she straddled the divides and chasms opening up in America at that time, yet she also remained somewhat peripheral to the fierce debates erupting. This was a time of youthful revolt which saw powerful protests against the Vietnam draft (conscription) and the civil rights movement. It was also the era of the Stonewall riots fighting for gay rights, and the Roe vs Wade case which overrode total bans on abortion then in place in some US states. But in some ways, Rand was in tune with the zeitgeist of Americans on the march. She was certainly supportive of a woman's right of mastery over her reproductive rights, and she also opposed the draft and the Vietnam War. Part of her message was about individual rights and a rejection of any imposed morality on consenting adults. She was also no supporter of racial segregation. Yet in other ways, her place in the 1960s was far more ambiguous and reactionary. She was vehemently anti-communist and opposed the whole notion of collective or group rights. She was a powerful advocate for unregulated free enterprise capitalism and, inasmuch as she backed any candidates for elected office, they were Republicans rather than Democrats. Her advocacy of a free market in both personal morality (whatever makes you happy and does not directly harm others), and in economics (greed is good in essence), make her something of a rather quirky figure in 1960s America. Here was a nation increasingly divided into 'peaceniks' and full-blown liberals seeking to bring greater equality to American society via a bigger state, and a conservative, patriotic anti-communist right who sought to restore 'true' American values, including in the area of morals and the central place for religion in public life. In an age of increasing unease, questioning and soul-searching, it is easy to see why Rand's work grew in popularity and why her views won a growing number of admirers.

One should also not neglect the somewhat nebulous impact of Hollywood culture. For Rand, the allure of what the 21st century terms 'celebrity culture', was also present. As a creative writer and thinker, she deliberately sought publicity and followers and spoke and broadcast regularly until her death.

Literary Influences

Any discussion of the influences on Rand's thinking cannot ignore the fact that she expressed her ideas primarily through her novels. The Frenchman Victor Hugo was her self-proclaimed literary hero from who she acquired the sense of the romantic novel, albeit one centred around the heroic figure. She commented that it was from the author of *Les Misérables* (1862) that she first grasped the concept of the grandeur of man. The heroic figure in Hugo's work (incidentally an even lengthier read than Rand's two principal novels), Jean Valjean, is a doer not a taker, and a man who often struggles against the system. While Rand had little time for Valjean's compassion and generosity to the poor, let alone his religious conversion experience, she did admire the character's command of his own destiny and entrepreneurship. Such themes were central to Rand's philosophy based as it was on rational individualism. She also owed a literary debt to the great Russian novelist Fyodor Dostoevsky (1821–1881) and his writing technique. She studied his novels carefully – *Crime and Punishment* (1866) being one example – in order to grasp how he integrated his ideas into his plots and what kinds of events express different themes in his works.

To Conclude

Ultimately, Rand was very much a product of a particular time and culture in both 20th century Russia and America. In her country of birth she experienced what it was to have riches taken away by the state. During her most formative years at Petrograd University, she began forming her political and philosophical ideas through the theories of Nietzsche, Aristotle, Aquinas and Marx, introduced to her by her professor, Lossky. Later, in her adopted country, she found the antithesis of the communism and authoritarianism that she had grown to hate in Russia, which propelled her to do everything in her power to keep it that way. In a land built around 'life, liberty and the pursuit of happiness', Rand sought to articulate and develop those themes in a manner appropriate to the fears yet also hopes of an America built upon capitalist sweat, dominated by Cold War era fears, and drifting towards an ever growing state. In many ways, these influences reinforced a zero sum non-dualist game for her. There was no halfway house or middle ground. It was liberty or enslavement, capitalism or state control, self-interest or self-surrender. By rejecting the extreme authoritarianism of the USSR and equally the spiritual mysticism of czarist Russia, she plumped for the opposite extreme instead. Rather like the evangelical Christian preachers she despised, it was a choice between heaven or hell, except salvation or damnation were found on this planet, and for this life only.

3. Philosophy of Objectivism

Without understanding the basic tenets of objectivism, one will fail to grasp anything else that Rand wrote or believed. To her and her followers, past and present, it is the essence of all her thinking and ideas condensed into one single all-encompassing system. It is something that must be viewed in its totality, not as individual and discrete units of thought. It was also very much intended for practical living, rather than for esoteric academic debate. In that sense, rather like Marxism or the systemic theology of Aquinas, it was a set of beliefs to be lived out in the real world. Also, like all builders of a philosophical system, it developed over time. Unusually, perhaps, for a philosopher and political thinker, the core ideas of objectivism are conveyed through Rand's novels. They are present in *The Fountainhead* but only became fully developed in *Atlas Shrugged*, particularly through the books' heroes, Howard Roark, Dagny Taggart and, above all, John Galt. Rand included key extracts from her novels in her non-fiction works, such as *For the New intellectual* and *Capitalism: The Unknown Ideal* (1966). Her non-fiction was largely her response to contemporary events like the Vietnam War and the American Civil Rights Movement, as well as a development of her approaches to epistemology and economics. Rand condensed objectivism into four clear but interlinked branches:

Metaphysics

Objective reality is all that matters and is all we can be certain about. Facts are facts and reality cannot be altered by wishes or emotion.

Epistemology

Human reason is the only source of knowledge, and applying reason is humanity's only way to survive. True knowledge therefore never comes through feelings.

Ethics

Self-interest trumps everything else. Men and women are ends in themselves, we exist for ourselves, not for others or for institutions such as the party, Church or state.

Politics

Unregulated free market capitalism is the only environment where all can be truly free and avoid ending up as masters or slaves. The government has a very limited role, staying out of the economy apart from defending property owners from theft and foreign invasion.

Rand made an impressive boast about her ideas. In her first televised interview with Mike Wallace in 1959 she claimed that 'I am primarily the creator of a new code of morality which has so far been believed impossible – namely, a morality not based on faith, not on emotion, not on arbitrary edicts, mystical or social, but on reason.' (Wallace, 1959). More modestly perhaps, in a

Playboy interview she explained how she wanted to 'Provide men – or those who care to think – with an integrated, consistent and rational view of life.' (Butler, 2018)

So what then are the key facets of objectivism properly understood, and how do they feature in her writing, above all her novels?

Metaphysics

A key strand to Rand's thinking is that we can, or at least should be, concerned only with what is objectively real. Facts are facts, whether we like them or not. Emotion, feelings or any notion of the supernatural or spiritual, are misplaced and misguided. As her protagonist in *Atlas Shrugged*, John Galt, phrases it, 'Existence exists – and the act of grasping that statement implies two corollary axioms [statements]: that something exists which one perceives and that one exists possessing consciousness, consciousness being the faculty of perceiving that which exists' (1957). The world we see is reality itself. We exist with the abilities or faculties to understand it and figure it all out, but we can only do so if we apply sufficient rational logic. Humankind therefore requires no divine revelations or holy texts to make sense of the world.

Many of the most important concepts in this area are found in John Galt's lengthy speech in *Atlas Shrugged* which, in many ways, is a summary of the key principles of objectivism. The following is an extract of that speech:

> *'Whatever you choose to consider, be it an object, an attribute or an action, the law of identity remains the same. A leaf cannot be a stone at the same time, it cannot be all red and all green at the same time, it cannot freeze*

and burn at the same time. A is A. Or, if you wish it
stated in simpler language: You cannot have your cake
and eat it, too.'

But Rand would also go further and posit that, although
identity is real and immutable, in order to understand why we
are as we are, our perception requires us to 'think and think
objectively' (Butler, 2018). This brings us on to the second aspect
of objectivism: the place of epistemology.

Epistemology

Rand's starting point is that the world is not self-revelatory, it
does not come with a user manual. Instead, we have to apply
logic and reason to make sense of it. To survive and flourish we
need to understand how and why things work, and to learn this
requires time and effort. We have to work out for ourselves what
terms such as 'business' or 'freedom' really mean. In Rand's own
words, some of the key aspects of 'how we know what we know'
can be summed up thus:

'Man is neither infallible nor omniscient; if he were,
a discipline such as epistemology—the theory of
knowledge—would not be necessary nor possible: his
knowledge would be automatic, unquestionable and
total. But such is not man's nature. Man is a being of
volitional consciousness [...] a level inadequate to the
cognitive requirements of his survival—man has to
acquire knowledge by his own effort, which he may
exercise or not, and by a process of reason, which he may
apply correctly or not. Nature gives him no automatic

guarantee of his mental efficacy; he is capable of error, of evasion, of psychological distortion. He needs a method of cognition, which he himself has to discover: he must discover how to use his rational faculty, how to validate his conclusions, how to distinguish truth from falsehood, how to set the criteria of what he may accept as knowledge.' (Rand, 1979)

In other words, the focus is on the individual to figure it out for themselves, to apply reason and logic to those deeper questions beginning with 'why' and 'what'. Hence the constant refrain in her writing on the role of the individual not the collective, and the need to think and reason for oneself. Her approach to knowledge and the application of reason also involves the dialectic process identified in Chapter 2. As one leading Rand scholar puts it, 'She sees a movement from creative thought to material production to exalted spiritual satisfaction' (Sciabarra,1995), namely those familiar themes of thesis, antithesis and synthesis. For Rand, thinking was not aimless contemplation but a springboard that would lead to a practical outcome which, in turn, would create personal fulfilment. To use a classroom example, I might dream about delivering a stimulating and creative lesson for all my students, but this requires me to actually go away and create the resources and planning with which to realise it. The end reward is genuine satisfaction of a job well done. The prime mover of individual human action is the ability to think and reason.

This hankering after reason and creativity is again reflected in her writings. Rand's heroes, the architect Howard Roark in

The Fountainhead and John Galt in *Atlas Shrugged*, are humans capable of original thought and ideas who are driven by logic, not whims. Howard Roark sums up Rand's belief in the individual over the collective as follows:

> *'There is no such thing as a collective brain. There is no such thing as a collective thought. An agreement reached by a group of men is only a compromise or an average drawn upon many individual thoughts. It is a secondary consequence. The primary act—the process of reason—must be performed by each man alone. We can divide a meal among many men. We cannot digest it in a collective stomach. No man can use his lungs to breathe for another man. No man can use his brain to think for another. All the functions of body and spirit are private. They cannot be shared or transferred.'* (1943)

Ethics

As mentioned earlier, Rand's thinking is meant to be both self-contained and a complete system. It is also intended to be applicable to life rather than merely a set of abstract principles. Like Marxism, or a religion, a thought system is to be lived out in the world. Life cannot be separated from reason, purpose and self-esteem. This means, therefore, that ethics and morality are a central part of objectivism. Altruism and human nature will be dealt with in detail in Chapter 4, but for now we will look at the core values of Objectivist ethics.

First, Rand believed that humans are not born with an innate sense of right or wrong. Morality has to be uncovered by reason and thought. She rejected the traditional conservative view of human nature as imperfect and in need of outside guidance (whether via traditional institutions or by a 'natural' ruling elite) and instead, veered more towards a classic liberal view of humanity as capable of possessing and exercising reason to confront any challenges. Yet she was not quite the conventional classical liberal either. Rand's fundamental view on human nature was that we are born tabula rasa, a blank slate: neither inherently good nor fundamentally flawed. This is an idea that can be traced back to Aristotle (see Chapter 2). All knowledge and 'instinct' are not naturally intuitive but come from experience. Life, quite simply, is what one makes of it. Humankind, in Rand's view, is an end in itself, not the means to the ends of others. We must exist for our own sake, she says, neither sacrificing ourselves to others nor sacrificing others to ourselves. The pursuit of rational self-interest and our own happiness is the highest moral purpose of life itself.

It is important to note that Rand did not intend this as a manifesto for reckless individual actions that ignored the interests of others. Rather, it is an idealistic view of humans as essentially self-interested yet also self-regulating. Self-interest in the Randian universe would always be rational. An illustration might be helpful here. I might wish emotionally and lustfully to conduct an illicit affair with my best friend's partner, but rational self-interest should conclude that my own wellbeing would be adversely affected. I would run the real risk of losing my own partner and my best friend. The key point is that, while other systems of thought and belief – especially those that are faith-based – would simply condemn such an action as inherently sinful or immoral, for Rand it would be against one's self-interest. Ethics, says Rand, have to be separated from raw emotions or feelings. Some of her sharpest criticisms in her novels are reserved for those characters who are 'whim-worshippers': those who act without thought, driven purely by subjective emotions. As she puts it in an interview with the *Playboy* magazine in 1964,

> *'What does it mean, to act on whim? It means that a man acts like a zombie, without any knowledge of what he deals with, what he wants to accomplish, or what motivates him. It means that a man acts in a state of temporary insanity. Is this what you call juicy or colorful? I think the only juice that can come out of such a situation is blood. To act against the facts of reality can result only in destruction.'* (cited in Ayn Rand Lexicon)

By contrast, Rand argues that, while emotions are natural and a given part of the human condition, they need to be linked and integrated with reason before we act. To quote John Galt again: 'Emotions are inherent in your nature, but their content is dictated by your mind.' (1957). It is about achieving a synthesis of emotion and mind.

Politics

The final key tenet of objectivism is what it has to say about politics, the nature of the state and capitalism. Rand expressed her key ideas very succinctly when she wrote,

> *'The ideal political-economic system is laissez-faire capitalism. It is a system where men deal with one*

another, not as victims and executioners, nor as masters and slaves, but as traders, by free, voluntary exchange to mutual benefit. It is a system where no man may obtain any values from others by resorting to physical force, and no man may initiate the use of physical force against others. The government acts only as a policeman that protects man's rights; it uses physical force only in retaliation and only against those who initiate its use, such as criminals or foreign invaders.' (Ayn Rand Lexicon)

What we have here is an endorsement of private enterprise and the defence of private property; a small state and limited government that carries out the minimum of roles such as national defence and the enforcement of contracts; and the centrality of individual rights. Rand's politics were very much based on rights and a very individual interpretation of these rights.

Rand is a difficult thinker to classify neatly into the conventional categories of conservative or liberal, although one can certainly discard the terms socialist and anarchist. This problem of classification can be seen time and again. In Andrew Vincent's *Modern Political ideologies* (1992), references to Rand are found in the liberalism chapter, whereas in Festenstein and Kenny's *Political Ideologies* (2005), her entry is found in the conservatism section, sandwiched between Friedrich Hayek and Margaret Thatcher (1925–2013). Her preferred term, inasmuch as she said anything about political labels, was a 'radical for capitalism' (Rand, 1966). So, is Rand best viewed as a liberal, a conservative or as something else entirely?

The most appropriate term, using conventional political labels albeit one that she despised, is probably that of libertarian: one who favours a maximum of individual freedom and a minimum of government interference. Yet it is important not to see her as a supporter of anarchism – a movement that promotes a state without any form of government – and to note that Rand herself rejected those who employed or misused her ideas to justify a completely stateless society. Rand writes in 1971:

> *'For the record, I shall repeat what I have said many times before: I do not join or endorse any political group or movement. More specifically, I disapprove of, disagree with and have no connection with, the latest aberration of some conservatives, the so-called "hippies of the right," who attempt to snare the younger or more careless ones of my readers by claiming simultaneously to be followers of my philosophy and advocates of anarchism [...] Anarchism is the most irrational, anti-intellectual notion ever spun by the concrete-bound, context-dropping, whim-worshiping fringe of the collectivist movement, where it properly belongs.'* (Ayn Rand Lexicon)

Why this tirade? Because, as previously noted, Rand believed that life was not about simply doing what one felt at any given moment, a licence to let one's emotions run freely. Instead, life is to be approached seriously and with purpose. Any right-thinking person, in her view, would want to respect the rights of others, and some functions of the state – such as enforcing the rights of property and resisting foreign aggression – necessitate the existence of some kind of minimalist government. What Rand would always reject is the concept of a big state that exists to redistribute wealth in the name of equality and fairness. The role of the state, she argued, is not to coerce the individual into a more 'virtuous' lifestyle, or financially through excessive and redistributive taxation. Her view on society was essentially atomistic not collective. As one of her characters in *The Fountainhead*, Hugh Akston, (John Galt's philosophy teacher) puts it, 'Man is a social being but not in the way that the looters preach' (1943). By this he means that the ideal Objectivist society is one where everyone mixes and gets on well with others, but as a voluntary association of self-interested individuals. What is rejected is any notion of inherent societal obligations and duties. In the words of the former British Prime Minister, Margaret Thatcher, in an interview for *Women's Own* in September 1987:

> *'Who is society? There is no such thing! There are individual men and women and there are families, and no government can do anything except through people and people look to themselves first. It is our duty to look after ourselves and then also to help look after our neighbour and life is a reciprocal business.'* (Margaret Thatcher Foundation)

While Thatcher was not a self-declared follower of objectivism, on this particular issue of society, she did adopt an Objectivist stance.

Objectivism is Individualism

Rand's view of human nature was also intensely individualistic. She vehemently rejected those philosophies such as One-Nation conservatism that emphasize an organic society and invisible bonds that bind together the generations. With equal, if not more, force, she also rejected any sense of the collectivism and communalism associated with socialism. There is no such thing as collective thought and group identity, Rand argued. She was also contemptuous of those who are content to live by the choices of others, who go along with the crowd, as well as those who seek power for its own sake, such as Ellsworth Toohey, the arch-villain in *The Fountainhead*.

To use a completely different analogy, most modern American sitcoms are created by a scriptwriting team, the idea being that individual writers all contribute, bounce ideas and jokes off one another, refine the lines and create a better, funnier script than would be possible individually. Communal activity by this measure has the effect of boosting creativity and productivity. Rand would consider this to be implausible: the end product would actually be worse not better, she would say, as it stifles the individual writer of genius who would be over-shadowed by 'lesser writers'. No wonder Rand always championed and lionized the creative genius of the individual who are the true heroes in her novels. In summary, when it comes to human nature, Rand emphasizes the power of positive thinking and of self-esteem. The Afterword to *Atlas Shrugged* highlights, 'The concept of man as a heroic being, with his own happiness as the moral purpose of his life, with productive achievement as his noblest activity, and reason as his only absolute.'

Rand's Novels

While the core of objectivism can be covered under the headings above, to make full sense of the term, and the ideas contained within it, requires some analysis of her dystopian novels. These were the main vehicle through which she popularized her ideas and Objectivist values. To know and appreciate her ideas, then, *The Fountainhead* and *Atlas Shrugged* are a good place to start.

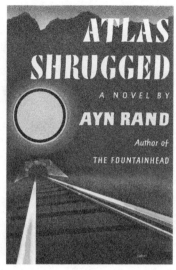

Rand wasn't the first author to use fiction as a way to verbalise political and philosophical beliefs. Her contemporary, British writer and essayist George Orwell (1903–50) –

Fig. 6 Rand's 1957 novel *Atlas Shrugged*.

best known as the author of *Animal Farm* (1945) and *Nineteen Eighty-Four* (1949) – also used this methodology. While their political ideas were far apart (Orwell was a socialist), both Orwell and Rand used novels set in the future to convey their wider messages. Their fictional characters (Winston Smith the propagandist in *Nineteen Eighty-Four* and Howard Roark in *The Fountainhead*) became mouthpieces for what the authors wanted to get across to their readers. Rand and Orwell also wrote their dystopian novels to warn against the all-powerful authoritarian state. Terms such as 'Big Brother' and 'Thought Police' originate from *Nineteen Eighty-Four*, while *Animal Farm* is a powerful indictment of Stalin's USSR. Rand's novels, though, are considerably longer than those of Orwell and in the opinion of most literary commentators, rather less well written.

Many powerful novels are about the struggle of the oppressed, the underdog fighting heroically against the wealthy and

Fig. 7 A Chicago sign displaying an often expressed question from Rand's novel *Atlas Shrugged*.

privileged, encouraging empathy for the poor and ill-treated. Rand's novels, however, are somewhat unusual in that they take a classic storyline and completely invert it. In *Atlas Shrugged*, it is the wealth creators and business owners, not the workers, who go on strike in protest against the ever expanding and grasping state. The book's opening line is the cryptic phrase, 'Who is John Galt?'. This becomes a common expression of helplessness and despair at the state of the novel's fictionalized world throughout the book. The line has also become a popular slogan among supporters of Rand's view, not least those Americans who want to shrink the state, such as the fiscally conservative Tea Party movement within the Republican Party.

Language and Characterisation

The titles of Rand's novels act to convey something of her ideas. *The Fountainhead* refers to the notion that it is the original or first-hand thinking of history's great creative minds that is the fountainhead of all human progress, as opposed to the mimicking or conformity of the 'second-handers' (the original title for the work); a 'second-hander' being one who merely apes or follows the ideas of others. *Atlas Shrugged*, meanwhile, is a reference to the Greek god Atlas who was punished by Zeus to bear the entire world on his shoulders. Rand's analogy stands in for the industrialists and geniuses of the world who essentially carry the entire planet by their brilliance and efforts, yet they are hated and envied. If they were to shrug off this weight, however, the world would literally fall to pieces.

As with many novelists, the leading characters in Rand's novels were sometimes inspired by real people. The archvillain in *The Fountainhead*, Ellsworth Toohey, was in part influenced by visits Rand made to hear the British political theorist and economist Harold Laski (1893–1950) speak. She even based some of her character's physical traits, such as an 'elegant slouch', on the real-life Laski. However, despite her best efforts, critics have generally agreed that Rand's characters are rather two-dimensional, lacking deeper emotions or complex characterisation. They are either heroes or villains, with no real place for more nuanced characters. One could argue that this is because Rand's books are, fundamentally, political tracts in novel form. They are mouthpieces for her own ideas of what is noble and heroic and what is not, rather than prose as an artform. Classic examples include Galt's 60-page speech in *Atlas Shrugged* and Howard Roark's defence speech in *The Fountainhead*. Both are largely channels through which Rand expresses her own ideas. If one wants to understand the basics of Rand's ideas, Galt's speech sums up much of it. Just as one can gain a good understanding of the basic premises of communism from reading the *Communist Manifesto* (1848), rather than wading through the far lengthier and more complex *Das Kapital* (1867), the same goes for Galt's speech (which, incidentally, is longer than Marx and Engel's entire *Communist Manifesto*). Galt's speech is essentially an amplification of the rather shorter defence statement by Howard Roark at the end of *The Fountainhead*. It contains phrases including 'No creator was prompted by a desire to serve his brothers', and 'Man cannot survive except through his mind. He comes on earth unarmed, his brain is his only weapon'. Again, this represents Rand's central emphasis on the power and potential of the human mind, guided solely by reason and rational self-interest. What mattered and counted most was the effort and determination of the gifted and talented.

Rand's portrayal of villains is also instructive. The principal 'bad guy' in *The Fountainhead*, Ellsworth Toohey, is an architectural critic and socialist who is ambitious and power hungry. Rand also portrays him as dangerous as he seeks to prevent others from excelling by teaching that talent and ability are of no great consequence, and that the greatest virtue is humility and charity. Rand gives him the withering description of being, 'a man who never could be, and knows it' (1943). Toohey is also represented as a man of the people; a populist who sets out to manipulate the masses and ultimately create a dictatorship. One of the most memorable lines given to him is: 'Great men can't be ruled. We don't want any great men.' Toohey represents the epitome of everything that Rand detested in humankind: a desire for total control over the lives and minds of others dressed up in the language of charity, the popular will and the common good. It is not just her heroes who are mouthpieces for her views, but their enemies, too.

In Summary

Rand's novels sold well and continue to do so. There is a strong sense that those who enjoy and engage with her novels are inherently drawn to much of her outlook and values. Those that find them unreadable and depressing, for the values and heroes they embrace, would doubtless reject objectivism as well. For those who view capitalist Western societies as structurally racist, elitist and patriarchal, her books will hold no attraction and, indeed, appear positively dangerous. Like objectivism itself, Rand's novels have a niche appeal and contain a mixture of both intriguing yet also problematic concepts and themes. To conclude, objectivism was created by Rand to primarily provide a guide to living, based on reason not emotion, and logic not superstition or inherited tradition. Centred on the individual and their own self-fulfilment, the characters in her novels convey both the essence of her ideas, and also what she most stood against. But what exactly did she have to say about morality, selfishness and altruism? The next chapter sets out to explain.

4. Individualism and Morality

While the four Objectivist branches of metaphysics, epistemology, ethics and politics form the bedrock of Rand's philosophy, probably the most well-known and often misunderstood aspect of her ideas concern her view on selfishness and its philosophical nemesis, altruism. But before these are explored in greater depth, one needs to appreciate further what she wrote and thought about human nature in order to fully make sense of what she meant by selfishness.

There is a complete absence in Rand's writing of any sense of a creator force or a deeper, more mystical, spiritual dimension to human existence. She saw mysticism or any kind of religious sentiment as based on a belief devoid of proof or objective reason. Rand also inverted the famous Cartesian dictum of 'I think therefore I am'. For her, it was more a case of 'I am, therefore I think'. The final page of her 1938 novella, *Anthem*, contains a rally cry for the sovereignty of the individual mind, 'I am, I think, I will.' At the heart of objectivism is the sense that humans only survive through the mind or, more precisely, the application of one's own mind. Much of the emphasis in Rand's writings and lectures is on this need to focus the mind by mobilizing our faculties of reason and thought when we contemplate an action or decision. In this sense, the follower of objectivism should be consciously 'flicking a switch' when it comes to deciding what to do or think.

If one were to ask Rand that most common of philosophical questions, 'What is the meaning of life?', her reply might be something along the lines of, 'simple survival': to stay alive and to live our best life is the goal by which we set our values. To an atheist like Rand there could be no question of reincarnation, and no rationale in seeing an earthly life as a preparation and test for eternal life. Values are determined by objective life-needs; that is, by the requirements of survival such as food or shelter. Values are therefore neither the intrinsic properties of things (the Platonic view) nor subjective and purely matters of preference, time or culture. Instead, values are relational or objective, dependent on the nature of the organism and the nature of its environment. What is right or 'good' is what aids us in our survival. Though, as will be noted later, Rand was far from advocating hedonism or unbridled libertarianism.

An example might be useful here. Suppose we take the value of friendship. A conventional view of friendship might be that we should always value our friends unless they betray us or let us down in a major way. Their 'value' is not affected by what we get out of that relationship. We stand by our friends and value them because they are just that: friends. To Rand's way of approaching this topic philosophically, the value of friendship is a variable. I might value a plumber friend more when they give me helpful advice on how to deal with a leaking tap, than at other times. In other words, value is dependent on context. It is also rational and logical, if mechanistic and self-centred. In her own words, she expressed it thus,

'To love is to value. Only a rationally selfish man, a man of self-esteem, is capable of love—because he is the only man capable of holding firm, consistent, uncompromising, unbetrayed values.' (Rand, 1964)

From a Randian perspective, friendship – and indeed love – is fundamentally and rightfully selfish. Ultimately it rests on self-preservation; on the value it adds to our own lives. The man who does not value himself cannot value anything or anyone. We make friends because we want to have someone to chat to in our leisure time, to accompany us to social functions or, if we perceive them as less physically attractive or stylish than ourselves, to make ourselves look better by contrast. Crucially, Rand would argue that the other party would also be entering into a compact of friendship for equally selfish reasons, and both parties are free to break off the friendship if they are not getting a 'good deal' (a clause that she frequently put into action with her own friendships, as we saw in Chapter 1). There is little room for sentiment or emotion in the Randian outlook on life. We adapt and survive, or not as the case may be, and our human relationships, ethics and values should reflect this.

Society and the State

Rand's ideas on society were clear, if controversial: she had a highly atomistic and individualistic view of society. Many strands of political thought go by the idea that society is natural and positive and, even for classical liberals such as John Locke (1632–1704) who, like Rand, emphasized both individual and property rights, society is a place where one is nourished and fed. Indeed, most anarchist thinkers, who reject the notion of a formal state, view society as a 'natural' part of the human condition. They see men and women as essentially communal, the only difference being that the order should come from within without being imposed by the state. But, for Rand, there is in one sense no such thing as society, merely an assortment of independent individuals who respect the rights of others while following their own philosophy or code of ethics. The only good is therefore the individual good. It is important to note, however, that Rand never advocated a society or state without any boundaries or regulations. For Rand's society to work at all – and of course it is debatable whether a strictly Randian society can even function, let alone produce fair (i.e. proportionate to individual effort and creativity) outcomes for all – it is imperative that everyone respects the individual rights of others.

This is why and where Rand contrasts with anarchists. Why should theft be punishable? Not because it breaks some invisible moral code handed down on tablets of stone, but because it infringes the creative and productive rights of another. The state's role, argues Rand, is necessarily small and should essentially only be concerned with enforcing laws necessary to the enjoyment of one's own property and rights. As Rand's hero John Galt puts it,

> *'The only proper purpose of a government is to protect a man's rights which means: to protect him from physical violence. A proper government is only a policeman, acting as an agent of man's self-defense, and, as such, may resort to force only against those who start the use of force. The only proper functions of a government are: the police, to protect you from criminals; the army, to*

protect you from foreign invaders; and the courts, to
protect your property and contract from breach or fraud,
to settle disputes by rational rules, according to objective
law.' (1957)

Rand believed that citizens require the peace guaranteed by
the state to create and produce in the first place and, thereafter, to
maintain ownership and enjoyment of the fruits of their labour.
A free and capitalist society therefore requires the organs of the
state to preserve the sacred rights of private ownership.

Morals and Altruism

Rand's worldview is intensely moralistic. Humans should act
morally, not out of formal obligation or fear of divine punishment,
she argues, but because their own individual rights, survival
and happiness depend upon it. In Rand's world, though, the
focus on the development of the self-sufficient ego means that
momentary pleasures and fleeting emotions are squeezed out in
favour of one's own striving and goals. There are often echoes
of J.S. Mill's (1806–73) 'higher and lower pleasures' in some of
Rand's writing; actions and morals that enhance us as rational
human beings. Rand regarded higher pleasures, such as building
up a successful business enterprise or creating a widely admired
work of art, as more valuable than lower pleasures that are purely
animalistic desires, such as eating something appetizing or
having sex. She considered these necessary acts as contributing
little or nothing. (Although, as we shall see later in this chapter,
Rand's Objectivist philosophy does in fact promote sex as rising
above lower pleasures because it embraces more noble elements
and virtues.)

Few aspects of Rand's writing have been as controversial as her views on altruism – an act which entails helping others out with no expectation of personal reward. Most philosophies and world faiths applaud this human generosity and kindness to others. But Rand rejected traditional altruism in favour of unabashed self-interest. Before investigating her views on the topic, it is worth knowing something of the origins and assumptions that underpin the normal endorsement of altruism in its broadest sense. It has three basic roots.

First, liberal and socialist thinkers would suggest that we should help others in need because it is just and fair. For philosophers such as T.H. Green (1836–82) or John Rawls, the emphasis is on the common good, working towards the abolition, or at least reduction, of poverty by some redistribution of wealth via taxes. Their school of thought argues that we all have shared responsibilities and duties towards each other if we are to create a fair and stable society. In such a world view, objective notions of justice and fairness compel humankind to 'look out' for others, something which inevitably involves a larger state and a major investment in public services.

Second, traditional conservative thinkers such as philosopher and economist Edmund Burke (1729–1797), would focus on the duties that inherited privilege and wealth brings with it. With this worldview, a benevolent paternalism pervades. Those at the top look after those less fortunate out of duty but also self-interest. Acts of charity, a nice food hamper at Christmas perhaps, these keep the masses happy and content and thereby avoids violent revolution. As the 19th century Tory politician and Prime Minister Benjamin Disraeli (1804–81) quipped, 'The palace is not safe when the cottage is unhappy' (Buckle &

Monypenny, 1910). In the hierarchical and ordered world of such thinkers and political actors, it is self-preservation along with moral responsibility that promotes altruistic, charitable actions.

Lastly, the moral teaching of the leading world faiths also comes into play when promoting altruism. Take one example from Christianity: in John's Gospel, Jesus is recorded as saying, 'My command is this: Love each other as I have loved you. Greater love has no one than this: to lay down one's life for one's friends' (John Ch 15 v12-13). Indeed, the whole notion of sacrificial love and loving one's neighbour runs rich throughout the Bible. One can see a similar emphasis on sacrificial love for a deity in Islam. Thus in the Quran one can read 'Surely my prayer and my sacrifice and my life and my death are all for Allah, the Lord of the worlds' (Ch 6 v162). Most traditional religious teachings encourage the believer to love a deity first, serve their fellow beings second and focus on oneself last. Pride and self-aggrandisement are firmly to be consigned to one side.

So why all this preamble before getting on to what Rand had to say about altruism? Simply because Rand was a disruptor, a revolutionary, and controversial in her philosophical rejection of the whole notion of self-sacrifice and conventional altruism. This advocacy of putting oneself first was enabled and emboldened by Rand's militant atheism. For her, religion – like totalitarian governments – reduces the true freedom of the individual. Credal beliefs impose morality on human beings, rather than letting a person develop their own code of values and ethics. In an interview, Rand sums up her egocentric view of humanity thus: 'Man exists for his own sake, that the pursuit of his own happiness is his highest moral purpose, that he must not sacrifice himself to others, nor sacrifice others to himself' (Rand, 2001). Nothing could be further from the altruism, service and sacrifice demanded by the deities of organized religion, or dictators seeking to create a heaven on earth. Nor, equally, does it resemble the call to collective action and sacrifice by leaders of democratic states in times of national crisis.

One of her most relevant writings in this area is *The Virtue of Selfishness*. Here, Rand seeks to make several key points:

- Selfishness properly understood is normal and correct. There is nothing more normal or natural than being concerned primarily with one's own interests first and foremost.

- Altruism, by contrast, is to be rejected as a virtue, as its true meaning is 'otherness'. Those who practise genuine altruism are not properly living or existing for themselves, but for others, which rather contradicts the whole purpose, in Rand's view, for existing at all.

Crucial to making full sense of what Rand means by both selfishness and altruism is the concept of the 'beneficiary of values'. Put simply, this means asking the question of who benefits from any given set of values. Rand explains:

> *Altruism declares that any action taken for the benefit of others is good, and any action taken for one's own benefit is evil. Thus the beneficiary of an action is the only criterion of moral value—and so long as that beneficiary is anybody other than oneself, anything goes.'* (1964)

What she was against was the idea that doing good for someone else's benefit is fundamentally the right thing. She argues that there is no objective moral superiority in helping someone else; it is simply subjective. Altruism is not automatically good or positive and it should certainly never be morally imposed on society. But how could this play out in practice? Take the example of helping a homeless person. The conventional definition of altruism would argue that giving that individual a sum of money or just a hot drink and a kind word would always be a moral positive in the eyes of society, a 'good' thing to do. If we follow Rand's line of reasoning, however, such an act of charitable giving is not a positive action. A gift of money could be spent on alcohol or drugs, perpetuating and subsidizing the problems of that individual. Even a gift of a hot coffee might lead to that individual scalding themselves if they were under the influence of drugs or drink. Finally, would a charitable act actually be counterproductive to the individual's long-term best interests by promoting a dependency rather than self-sufficient syndrome? The key point here is that altruism is not self-evidently morally superior or 'right'.

It is important to note that Rand was not arguing that we should be unpleasant or uncaring to others, but rather that the philosophical basis for altruism is flawed. Those who live their lives in the interests of others, or who just go along with the prevailing view, are thought to be self-less, which essentially translates as 'non-person'. If giving money or aid makes us feel better, then that's fine. If I purchase some fine fillet steak at the supermarket, I might genuinely want to buy some cheap food items for the local foodbank so I feel better about my expensive dinner. According to Rand, there is nothing wrong with this form of altruism, but it must come from an act of genuinely wanting to; of according with one's own chosen code of values. There should be no wider moral imperative or 'guilt trip' involved, and certainly no governmental coercion. To take the analogy slightly further, the ultimate injustice for Rand would be a state where a law requires the purchasers of all 'luxury' food items to also donate to those experiencing food poverty.

Rand's Approach to Selfishness

How can we best understand what Rand meant by the term selfishness? On the one hand it goes against many of the traditional moral values instilled in us as children: think of others first, wait your turn and help others less fortunate than yourself. Taken to its logical conclusion, it hardly seems to be a recipe for a caring, sharing world. Ethical egoism, we might suppose, would struggle to understand an individual such as the Roman Catholic saint and priest Maximilian Kolbe (1894–1941). An inmate in the Auschwitz concentration camp during WWII, he volunteered to be executed in place of a fellow prisoner who had a family. From an Objectivist standpoint, this seemingly flies in the face of ethical egoism, but a Randian response to this might well be that Kolbe was in fact acting out of rational self-interest from his own standpoint. By committing an act of supreme self-sacrifice, giving up his life for another, he was enhancing his prospect of heavenly reward in the afterlife.

Objectivism, rightly or wrongly, does tend to reduce the motivation behind human actions to a fairly cynical level. On the other hand, it also raises some uncomfortable questions surrounding our motives and choices. For example, how far are love and friendship transactional and based around mutual benefit? How self-centred are we, even when we claim to be acting altruistically? Rand would argue, emphatically, that we should never act purely in the interests of another and equally that we should never expect or cajole others to act purely for our self-interest. One of the most famous quotes in *Atlas Shrugged* is John Galt's oath, when he says, 'I swear, by my life and my love of it, that I will never live for the sake of another man, nor ask another man to live for mine.' One can clearly see here an inversion of the biblical injunction cited previously concerning laying down one's life for others. Yet the notion of a pledge does also convey the sense that Rand viewed objectivism as something profound, deep and heroic. Ironically, it almost resembled a monastic vow in part. It was a promise to live one's life rationally eschewing emotion, emotionalism and collectivism, and instead embrace a vision involving living purely for oneself following one's own chosen principle. The final word on altruism and selfishness though should go to Rand herself:

> '*The issue is whether the need of others is the first mortgage on your life and the moral purpose of your existence. The issue is whether man is to be regarded as a sacrificial animal. Any man of self-esteem will answer:* "*No.*" *Altruism says:* "*Yes.*"' (Rand, 1982)

Love and Sex

One particularly interesting aspect of objectivism is how it depicts love and sex. The picture is somewhat complex and Rand's own private life and affair, covered later on, tend to muddy the waters somewhat. Selfishness in the Randian sense is the key starting point here. As we have already established, for Rand, to be selfish is merely acting rationally. Seeking our own self-interest is the most natural and logical thing in the world for the individual that has any self-respect for themselves. Yet Rand was no advocate of free love or promiscuity. She writes:

> 'Sex is one of the most important aspects of man's life and, therefore, must never be approached lightly or casually. A sexual relationship is proper only on the ground of the highest values one can find in a human being. Sex must not be anything other than a response to values. And that is why I consider promiscuity immoral. Not because sex is evil, but because sex is too good and too important.'
> (Rand, 2001)

Once again, we see the importance of a life driven by values, self-esteem and logic, not lust and emotion. Rand's approach to marital affairs was interesting. She would not embrace the view of social conservatives that extramarital affairs are wrong because they are intrinsically immoral. Instead, her approach was more nuanced:

> 'I think the question of an affair or a marriage depends on the knowledge and the position of the two persons involved and should be left up to them. Either is moral, provided only that both parties take the relationship seriously and that it is based on values.' (Rand, 2001)

Yet, ironically, Rand appears to have found this hard to put into practice in her own private life, for example, when her affair with

Nathaniel Branden ended and he became attracted to another, younger woman. One would assume that Rand, as a rational and objective thinker, would have accepted Branden's decision. After all, if we follow Rand's own line of thinking, he was acting out of self-interest. Instead, Rand's reaction was more typical of a 'lover spurned', although she would probably have argued that Branden was acting out of irrational sexual desire. In *The Virtue of Selfishness*, she says that man's right to act for his own rational self-interest 'is not a license to "do as he pleases" […] nor to any man motivated by irrational emotions, feelings, urges, wishes or whims'. One presumes that Branden did not view it in quite the same way. Perhaps human nature is a little more emotional and internally inconsistent than even objectivism's supreme spokesperson would have us believe.

Philanthropy and Surplus Wealth

What would Rand make of the generous philanthropy of a self-made multi-billionaire such as Bill Gates (b.1955)? We can surmise that she would have no problem with him giving away the bulk of his vast wealth if that was what he genuinely wanted to do and if it brought him additional happiness. But, in the particular case of Gates, she might well question his motivation. In their 10th Annual Letter, issued in 2018, Bill and Melinda Gates explain that the creation of a charitable foundation is 'a basic responsibility of anyone with a lot of money. Once you've taken care of yourself and your children, the best use of extra wealth is to give it back to society' (Clifford, 2018). The whole notion of any imposed moral obligation to give away one's honestly created wealth was anathema to Rand. Fascinatingly, there is an almost exact parallel to the Gates' perspective in *Atlas Shrugged*, spoken by one of the villains in the novel, James Taggart, who says, 'it is time to forget your selfish greed and give some thought to your social responsibilities, because I think that all those millions you're going to inherit are not for your personal pleasure, they are a trust for the benefit of the underprivileged and poor' (1957). Rand rejected the whole notion of vicarious responsibility, being morally obliged or beholden to the material needs of others.

Much harder, though, is to ascertain what exactly Rand would argue should happen to such vast surplus wealth. Clearly she would not advocate it being taken away by the taxman, but should it simply be spent on more private jets, yachts and private holiday retreats? Where does rational free choice to help others end, and a sense of moral obligation begin? A tricky issue for Objectivists, albeit one that few of us face in reality. There is no endorsement in objectivism for 'conspicuous consumption' and a vulgar hedonism. Indeed the whole notion of keeping up with the Joneses and having more supercars and yachts than one's rivals is rather at odds with the Objectivist belief in setting one's own goals and not simply conforming to a role. It has as much to do with training the mind as with accumulating vast wealth, though the latter is of course morally acceptable if it is down to one's own creative energy and genius. This represents, perhaps, one of the harder aspects of objectivism to resolve: that the rich be under any moral duty to share their wealth with the less fortunate. In 'What is Capitalism' (1966) Rand wrote,

'"The common good" (or "the public interest") is an undefined and undefinable concept: there is no such entity as "the tribe" or "the public"; the tribe (or the public or society) is only a number of individual men.'

From such a position, Rand discarded the whole notion of surplus wealth; Surplus to whom? she would ask. A person's property is theirs to enjoy in whatever way most brings them fulfilment. Society and the 'common good' certainly has no claim upon it. The following chapter will look at Rand's attitude towards capitalism in more depth.

5. Capitalism and Politics

In the late 1980s, British comedian Harry Enfield (b.1961) created the fictional character 'Loadsamoney' to epitomize and satirize the growth of popular capitalism and glorification of wealth during the years when Margaret Thatcher was British Prime Minister from 1979–90. Rand, not an individual known for her sense of humour, would have seen nothing particularly ironic about this comedy character. For Rand, the creation and celebration of wealth by one's own work and honest endeavours was indeed something to shout and sing about, as is evident in *Atlas Shrugged*, which is full of the ostentatiously rich. Where the novels of Dickens take us into the urban slums of Victorian England, those of Rand transport us to glamorous five-star hotels and luxury abodes. US President Franklin D. Roosevelt's 'forgotten man', whose plight he highlighted in one of his 1932 'fireside chats' (a series of evening radio addresses) explaining the New Deal, is pretty much just that in Rand's tales – forgotten.

As we have already encountered, Rand embraced a free market and a no-holds-barred capitalism with the same vehemence with which she detested collectivism and communism. According to Rand, 'Capitalism is a social system based on the recognition of individual rights, including property rights where all property is privately owned' (1966). Vigorously defending this statement, she goes on,

> '*Capitalism was the only system in history where wealth was not acquired by looting, but by production; not by force, but by trade, the only system that stood for man's right to his own mind, to his work, to his life, to his happiness, to himself.*'

Here, one can clearly recognize the Objectivist primacy of the individual and their rights to be creative, productive, and to enjoy the fruits of their labour. Rand's experience of the Bolsheviks seizing and nationalizing her father's pharmacy during the Russian Revolution (see Chapter 1) clearly influenced her beliefs on this point.

Rand viewed capitalism and altruism as being entirely incompatible. She shared the same beliefs in economic rights as all conservative political thinkers: above all, this includes the right to possess and enjoy one's own property and goods, lawfully gained, without interference or confiscation by the state in the name of equality or social justice. As one of her later biographers puts it: 'She wrote the recipe for deregulation' (Weiss, 2013). Wealth redistribution was abhorrent to Rand. Yet she went beyond traditional arguments when defending capitalism. Most notably in *Capitalism: The Unknown Ideal* – the collection of essays penned by both herself and fellow Objectivist collaborators including Alan Greenspan and Nathaniel Branden – she claimed a more radical and moral justification for capitalism. The 'unknown ideal' was her contention that most people outside her Objectivist circle did not really understand what capitalism represented. Wealth creation was another dimension of rational self-interest in the pursuit of survival and individual flourishing. She argued that state and the economy should be separate, rather as religion and the state are in the USA. Beyond a minimal state that enforces the criminal code against theft, individuals and businesses should be free to operate unhindered by the state.

Fig. 8 Objectivist philosopher, Leonard Peikoff, heir to Rand's estate.

Peikoff, in his (Rand-authorized) analysis of objectivism, explains it as follows: 'In a free market, there are no government controls over the economy. Men act freely and voluntarily, by individual choice and free trade.' (Piekoff, 1993)

The Free Mind

For Rand, the free capitalist economy was an outworking of the mind's creative freedom which she advocated in all other aspects of objectivism. A free market and a free mind went hand in hand with one another. Rand emphasized the mutual but necessarily voluntary free trading of gifts, skills and products. To take the example that Rand herself made: to one person, a piece of flint is useless; to a creative individual with the right skillset it can be fashioned into an arrowhead for hunting. But one can't live off arrowheads so the survival instinct leads the arrowhead maker to trade it for a pot so that they can cook their food; and the pot maker can use the arrowhead for hunting, as a pot is useless unless there is food to cook. The crucial thing for Rand is that both parties feel they have exchanged something of a lower value for something of a higher value. Therefore, she says, capitalism works for both parties.

Also key to this theory is that the deal is entered into voluntarily, with those creating the original product retaining ownership until they freely trade it for another more desirable (in their eyes) item. In pursuit of survival, we might add that, if the demand for flint arrowheads, or indeed pots, disappears (for example, because someone makes metal spears that are better for hunting) then the flint arrowhead creator adapts and innovates. This is why, Rand argues, capitalism is the only rational system that enables humankind to survive and progress. Again, the emphasis is on applying individual reason to the challenge of survival.

Rand also dismisses the notion of a mixed economy – a blend of capitalism and public ownership that was increasingly common in many Western democracies during the 20th century. In her view, this would inevitably lead to statism – the growth of the all-powerful state. Rand believed that, when it comes to the economy and capitalism, there is an element of Darwinism and its theory of 'survival of the fittest', albeit that she was referring to those who (in her opinion) are mentally fit – led by reason and individual egoism – rather than the physically most able. While she saw animals guided by instinct in pursuit of survival, she saw humans as uniquely blessed with the capacity to reason and to think freely.

Justification and Critiques

Rand seeks to justify capitalism not on efficiency grounds but on rational and moral grounds. Capitalism, in her opinion, is productive precisely because it involves free thought and independence. Human nature is both innately creative and self-centred. It is thus morally wrong to impede or steal the full fruits of that labour or ingenuity. Rand's economic outlook can be summed up as 'selfishness is both good and natural'. It is what makes us work harder, innovate and achieve fulfilment. Hardly surprising then, that this position has come under attack.

First, this support for the unfettered free market brings with it the danger of monopolies which, ironically, often stifle individual creativity and small independent businesses. Critics of unrestricted capitalism point to the fact that when a business or product gains a near monopoly in the marketplace, akin to a cartel, it often starts to abuse its position by increasing prices to enhance profits, once they have made it very hard for upstart competitors to break into the market and compete equally. Rand, arguably naively, had complete faith in the self-regulation of the market, believing that any monopoly was created in the first place through merit and only sustained through constantly staying 'ahead of the game'. In our modern age, dominated especially by a handful of tech giants such as Microsoft, Google, Facebook or Amazon, such a rose-tinted view seems rather harder to sustain. Can another creative IT genius really set up a business model that can challenge and genuinely compete with these technology titans? The odds are, to say the least, somewhat stacked against them, especially as so much of the software knowledge and programs/algorithms are effectively copyrighted for understandable commercial reasons. The initial financial resources required to compete would be vast, hence the reason that supporters of greater competition in this sector tend to look to governments to intervene and break up such near monopolies. It is not quite the same, one could argue, as setting up a rival market stall or even another automotive factory.

In addition, and somewhat personally for Rand herself as it turned out, there is also the issue of what happens when financial hardship strikes. Rand suffered serious bouts of illness in later life, including lung cancer brought on by heavy smoking. Faced with increasingly heavy and potentially crippling medical bills from America's largely private healthcare system, she was persuaded by a social worker and consultant to her publisher, Eva Pryor, to take social security and Medicare to avoid possible financial ruin. Some sources suggest she may have received as much as $11,000 from social security between 1974 and 1978 (Heller, 2009). Ironic, seeing as Rand taught that there was no such thing as the public interest, that programs like Social Security and Medicare steal from 'creators' and illegitimately redistribute their wealth. In effect, the taxpayers of America paid for Rand's medical expenses. Rand herself would no doubt have pointed to her argument on 'restitution' in a 1966 essay, 'The Question of Scholarships'. Essentially her justification would be that taking such state aid was not a social entitlement (in Rand's world no one 'owes' anyone anything) but was simply reclaiming 'stolen property'. In other words, taxes 'seized' by the authorities in more prosperous times. To many, though, this episode in her life reveals the shortcomings in her analysis of capitalism and of her ideas in general. In situations of crisis and dire need, we can be forced, however unwillingly, to face up to the fact that we need outside help and, most often in Western societies, that involves the state. Reason and self-interest will only get a person so far. Sometimes, as Rand herself experienced, the state can be a saviour instead of a fiend, as it was for Rand herself in her final years.

In our world today, Rand's view of a free-market capitalist economy is certainly problematic. Consider environmentalism: arguably, under the tenets of objectivism, the exploitation and pollution of the earth in our lifetime presents no issues because, morally, we owe nothing to future generations, only to ourselves and the present age. If the full implications of global warming and rising sea levels only affect future generations then why, with a strict reading of objectivism, should we care? A set of ideas centred only around oneself has little to say about modern issues such as long-term sustainability and any wider social responsibility. Extraction and exploitation of the Earth's resources have no real checks and balances beyond the short-term. One might well wonder what place a notion such as bio-diversity has in Rand's worldview.

Of course, if Rand were alive and active today, she is unlikely to be the same Rand of 20th-century America. She was writing well before the full consequences of man's degradation of the Earth and its natural resources were fully understood. Carbon emissions and climate change were not prime concerns during her era. Objectivism, as it was understood almost in the 1950s and '60s, could not work in today's society with all of our world problems. An altruistic stance towards future generations yet to be born is of paramount importance if those who come after us are to survive. It is certainly food for thought to wonder how Rand might have philosophized on our current predicament. Her hero, John Galt, is depicted in *Atlas Shrugged* as the inventor of a revolutionary electrostatic motor for cars so, perhaps unwittingly, Rand was pitching for environmentalism after all!

Race, Slavery and Working Conditions

Rand was highly critical of those countries with alternative regimes to the USA. There are many examples in her writings where she heaps withering prose on states such as China, the USSR, Cuba and Nazi Germany: all dictatorships based upon the servitude of the masses for the 'good' of the state and an ideological system. Absent from her critique, however, is how the USA and its capitalist system was, at least in part, built upon the enslavement of Black peoples from Africa. In fact, and controversially for many, she argued that capitalism actually helped abolish slavery. In her essay 'Racism', Rand writes:

> '*Capitalism is the only system that functions in a way which rewards rationality and penalizes all forms of irrationality, including racism [...] A fully free, capitalist system has not yet existed anywhere. But what is enormously significant is the correlation of racism and political controls in the semi free economies of the nineteenth century. Racial and/or religious persecutions of minorities stood in inverse ratio to the degree of a country's freedom. Racism was strongest in the more controlled economies, such as Russia and Germany — and weakest in England, the then freest country of Europe.'*
>
> *It is capitalism that gave mankind its first steps toward freedom and a rational way of life. It is capitalism that broke through national and racial barriers, by means*

*of free trade. It is capitalism that abolished serfdom
and slavery in all the civilized countries of the world.
It is the capitalist North that destroyed the slavery
of the agrarian-feudal South in the United States.'*
(Rand, 1964)

Her many critics would counter that analysis, not least by
arguing that it was precisely capitalism and the push for profit
that created the transatlantic slave trade in the first place. There
is also the profound moral issue that even if, and it is a big if,
capitalism would eventually eliminate slavery and promote racial
justice, can this in any way morally justify an economic system
that produced human suffering on a vast scale as part of its
evolutionary development?

It is important to note here that Rand was no racist. In the 1950s
and 60s when many conservatives, especially in the South, were
open supporters of racial segregation, she condemned racism as
the lowest, 'most crudely primitive form of collectivism' (1963).
She was also strongly against any form of racial predestination,
rejecting widely held views about the supposed characteristics of
certain races. Indeed, she saw crude racial stereotyping as, more
often than not, coming from those southerners who were widely
termed at the time as 'cheap white trash'. Rand was uninterested
in crude nationalism or notions of racial supremacy; she valued
only the individual, regardless of colour. But she also rejected any
notion of special rights or restitution for those disadvantaged or
discriminated against. She believed that the best way to combat
racism was via economic boycott or social ostracism, not wider
government action. Any notions of group action – minority

groups uniting together to fight for justice and equality – smacked to her of the collectivism she generally despised. For Rand, property rights always trumped civil rights.

There is one other cautionary note to make regarding Rand and the sensitive topic of race. Later in life, Rand became a supporter of the state of Israel, although it had nothing to do with religious or racial sentiment. Rather, as Weiss explains (2013), it was because she saw Israel as an outpost of Western 'civilization' in the Middle East and she considered the Arabs as 'among the least developed cultures' who were 'practically nomads'. It would seem that she perhaps saw all people as individuals, but some as more worthy of individualism than others.

The Role of the State

How far (if at all) should a state intervene to ensure safe working practices in factories? Many would say that, while capitalism can be beneficial, it can also lead to evils and exploitation, especially if left unchecked. Rand makes her views on this clear in her novels.

In *Atlas Shrugged*, the whole notion of revolution is entirely inverted. There is an economic depression going on with declining sales and profits for factories and businesses. But rather than the workers going on strike against their bosses in pursuit of higher wages or better working conditions, it is the inventors and capitalists who quit and disappear to an isolated valley called Galt's Gulch. This alternative utopian community, where no spongers are allowed, was created by John Galt, a successful motor engineer and inventor. Faced with the nationalisation of the factory, Galt disappears and effectively sabotages the production for the revolutionary new motor he has invented.

In *The Fountainhead*, the hero-protagonist Howard Roark is an innovative and intransigent architect who plays a major part in designing the prestigious Cortlandt housing project. He insists that no changes are to be made to his design and construction methods but is opposed by those that he calls 'second-handers', who value conformity over independent thinking. When he discovers that major changes have been made to his design, he dynamites the whole building. In court, following his defence speech, he is found not guilty. The moral of Rand's story is that Roark is regarded as a hero for sticking by his principles and for his willingness not to go along with 'groupthink' or simply swim with the current of public opinion. Although the subject of capitalism itself is less directly touched upon in *The Fountainhead*, in both books Rand's heroes are creative disruptors who rage against oppression by government and the 'second-handers', and who win.

Marx and Engels saw an evil determinism in capitalism, which must always be inherently exploitative. Rand shared a similar rigid determinism but in the opposite direction. Collectivism and opposition to free-market capitalism always ends in mediocracy and underachievement. Only self-reliance and individual effort rewarded by a capitalist economy, she argues, can bring true happiness and meaning.

Inequalities and Their Cause

A final area to critique regarding Rand's adulation of capitalism as she defined it, is the issue of structural inequalities. Rand's world is very much made up of heroic creators and producers; capitalist Stakhanovites (hero-workers in Stalinist Russia). But this world assumes that everyone is starting from the same point. How one runs the race to success depends on how fast and energetically one runs, it depends on one's own effort and commitment. Yet critics of such an approach would argue that the race is frequently rigged. Studies by many academics and groups, including the Center for American Progress in the USA and the Sutton Trust in the UK, have found that factors including family wealth and background, ethnicity, educational opportunities, gender and geography explain why achievement is not always the result of individual unaided effort. For Rand's philosophy to be fully consistent, there would have to be death duties of 100% which would effectively re-set the wealth (and hence advantages) to zero for each generation. This would prevent anyone from achieving a contented, prosperous life without putting in their own efforts. Otherwise, where is the incentive or requirement for someone with inherited wealth to be creative beyond some vague sense of intellectual satisfaction and fulfilment?

Yet Rand's philosophy forbids any notion of such redistributive taxation by the state. She would have argued that there would be little incentive in producing wealth if one knew that, ultimately, it could all end up in the hands of the state. A Catch-22 scenario then for those who believe in the absolute rights of private property, yet who also advocate the centrality of self-help and initiative. The outcome has to be that inherited, as opposed to self-created, inequality perpetuates itself. Society therefore consists of a self-perpetuating wealthy elite for who the playing field is surely tilted in their favour. Would a John Galt Jr (to be clear, no such character appears in the novel), have had the incentive or motivation to follow in his father's illustrious, creative and venerable footsteps? And if not, how does society convince him?

Even Rand's own life story is somewhat problematic on this score. In her afterword in *Atlas Shrugged*, she comments 'No one helped me, nor did I think it was anyone's duty to help me'. Yet the reality was rather more complicated. As one relatively recent biography (Heller, 2009) points out, she had many people who helped her in her early days, such as her Chicago relatives and Isabel Paterson. Rand did not quite make her own way in the world without at least a little help from her friends, though she was often less keen to acknowledge that publicly.

Democracy and Force

What should one make of Rand and her politics more widely? She was rabidly anti-socialist and anti-communist, passionately small state, free-market capitalism, and opposed to a code of ethics based on faith and sacred texts such as the Bible. Her ideas did not clearly align with either of America's two main parties. The Democrats were too associated with expanding state welfare programs and big government. While the Republicans were increasingly too influenced by the 'moral majority' agenda of the evangelical right with its anti-abortion emphasis and hostility to individual freedom in areas of sexual morality and promoting prayer in schools. Rand did, though, endorse the ultra-conservative Republican, Barry Goldwater (1909–98), in his 1964 campaign when he lost by a landslide against Lyndon B. Johnson (1908–73).

When it comes to democracy and the will of the majority, Rand appears somewhat conflicted. On the one hand, she fiercely denounced all forms of authoritarianism and believed in freedom of choice. Yet she also found it problematic in some ways, given her tendency towards elitism. Certainly some of her protagonists, such as Galt and Roark, possess almost superhero qualities. While not constituting a super-race, they are certainly part of an elite based around creativity, resolve and reason. Like the Founding Fathers of the American constitution, Rand had something of an inherent distrust of the masses. Were the masses truly capable of allowing the greatest and best to flourish? In *Atlas Shrugged*, for example, the democratic state is portrayed negatively and as an obstacle to the heroes of the story, including Galt, Taggart and Reardon. In the first part of the novel, a law called the Equalization of Opportunity Bill is passed. This forces large successful companies to break themselves up into smaller entities, similar to a lot of anti-trust legislation that was actually passed in the United States, such as the 1890 Sherman Act and the Clayton Act of 1914. The fictional act is passed by a majority of Congress and Rand's capitalist heroes are forced to sell off some of their businesses. The implication is that the legislation could only have been dreamt up by those who hate success, and yet it is 'those' who have been put in power by the people. The message, then, is that in the peoples' misguided pursuit of equality and fairness, democracy damages the rightful entitlement of wealth-creators.

Another of Rand's semi-contradictions is that, while opposing all forms of coercion and dictatorship – at least by the state – there is an admiration of raw force in other aspects. Such a quality is seen almost as an extension of the iron-will to succeed. In *Atlas Shrugged*, Dagny Taggart's heroic ancestor, Nathaniel Taggart, built a transcontinental railroad system almost single-handedly. Yet the novel also references, without condemnation, how he murdered a state legislator who was going to pass a law that would have stopped him from completing his railway. He also threw a government official down three flights of stairs for offering him a loan. In the world of *Atlas Shrugged*, these are depicted as noble and heroic acts. One gets the impression that Rand did not really trust democracy, hence why a minimal state was preferable. If government has limited power then it should make little difference who is in power. In her novels, violence is only portrayed negatively when it is sanctioned by the state, for example to confiscate the goods of the wealthy via law and taxation. Those in power are portrayed as a group who live second-hand lives (without individually creating anything of value), as they are dependent for their power on the support and popularity of others. While Rand detested all forms of dictatorship – fascist and communist – she also had little time for conventional democracy. If the state is minimalist and individual liberty is sacrosanct, then people need only a 'nightwatchman' to protect their rights.

Sexual Politics

One particularly interesting aspect in Rand's novels is her portrayal of women. No one could ever really call Rand a feminist writer, yet her female characters are not without sympathetic and positive portrayal. In her main novels there are powerful female characters, such as Dominique Francon in *The Fountainhead*, and Dagny Taggart in *Atlas Shrugged*, who runs Taggart Transcontinental, the largest and most successful transcontinental railroad in the country. None of Rand's heroines sacrifice their interests, intellect or values for the man or men in their life. Her women are independent, free-thinking and autonomous individuals. However, there is also a strong sense that Rand's fictional women need a man who is worthy of their hero-worship based on their values and principles. Rand seems to feel that this is what all women really desire. Her strong female characters are essentially defined by their relation to their (male) heroes.

Perhaps the most problematic and difficult aspect of how heroines are depicted in Rand's novels is the area of sexual consent. There is a particularly infamous scene in *The Fountainhead* where Francon invites Roark to come to her room and fix her fireplace, but things escalate after his second visit and he ends up raping her. One short extract from this scene reads as follows:

> *'She fought like an animal. But she made no sound [...]*
> *She reached for the lamp on the dressing table. He knocked*
> *the lamp out of her hand. [...] he had thrown her on to*
> *the bed and she felt the blood beating in her throat, in her*
> *eyes, the hatred, the helpless terror in her blood.'* (1943)

This certainly represents an act of non-consensual sex. Yet, when questioned about this scene, Rand argued that Francon desired this outcome, the clear implication being that she had 'wanted it' all along. Yet this analysis is highly problematic from our modern standpoint, in light of the #MeToo movement and the rightful emphasis on consent. Rand appears to portray her hero as taking a 'no-means-yes' approach to sexual activity. In a climate where there is much discussion of toxic masculinity and sexual violence, the predatory alpha-male heroes of Rand's novels jar badly in the light of current concerns.

Of course, Rand did not condone rape. In reply to a reader's question about the scene and published in the *Letters of Ayn Rand*, she replied thus:

'I am afraid that you have misunderstood Dominique in a very improper way. You write as if you thought that the lesson to be derived from it is that a man should force himself on a woman, and that she would like him for that. But the fact is that Roark did not actually rape Dominique; she has asked for it, and he knew that she wanted it. A man who would force himself on a woman against her wishes would be committing a dreadful crime. What Dominique liked about Roark was the fact that he took responsibility for their romance and for his own actions.' (Berliner, 1995)

So perhaps not rape so much as consensual sadomasochistic sex? Whatever Rand had in mind, the way she portrays gender relations makes for uncomfortable reading. There is certainly a sense in which her heroines, while strong and far more capable than many of the male characters in her novels, still hanker after 'real men' who are strong, tough and dominant. Of course, we are looking at these scenes from a contemporary perspective. Rand wrote in a culture deeply charged with sexist attitudes and stereotypes so, in many respects, her female characters are progressive for their era, even if they are simultaneously flawed from many perspectives.

While addressing Rand and feminism, it is worth briefly considering her broader attitude to gender role models. While fully embracing equality of intellect and reason between men and women, and also strongly defending a woman's right to control her own reproduction, Rand was also somewhat traditional in other areas. In 1968 she wrote 'An Answer to Readers (About a Woman President)', which included the following passage in response to how she would view a female US president:

> *'To act as the superior, the leader, virtually the ruler of all the men she deals with, would be an excruciating psychological torture. It would require a total depersonalization, an utter selflessness, and an incommunicable loneliness; she would have to suppress (or repress) every personal aspect of her own character and attitude; she could not be herself, i.e., a woman; she would have to function only as a mind, not as a person, i.e., as a thinker devoid of personal values—a dangerously artificial dichotomy which no one could sustain for long. By the nature of her duties and daily activities, she would become the most unfeminine, sexless, metaphysically inappropriate, and rationally revolting figure of all: a matriarch.'* (Ayn Rand Lexicon)

This traditional psychological attribution of female and male characteristics has unsurprisingly won Rand few friends among feminists, with American feminist journalist and author, Susan Brownmiller, calling her 'a traitor to her own sex' (1975).

The Legacy of Rand's Ideas

Although the legacy of Rand's writings on sexual politics has largely fallen out of favour today, not least with women, her broader ideas – especially on government and the economy – continue to attract many followers. Rand's celebration of capitalism found many disciples in the USA, not least among the wealthy and self-made. Not noted for his devouring of books, Donald Trump (b.1946) proclaimed himself a fan of *The Fountainhead* on his presidential campaign trail in 2016. He remarked 'It relates to business, beauty, life and inner emotions. That book relates to... everything.' (Freedland, 2017)

Endorsement and support for her views on deregulation and low taxes, small government and self-help, pre-date the 46th President of the United States, however. They became key mantras in the era of Republican

Fig. 9 Rand's 1943 novel *The Fountainhead*.

President Ronald Reagan's America (1981–89) and also impacted many Democrats, too. While it was Reagan who appointed one of Rand's early followers, Alan Greenspan, as chairman of the US Federal Reserve in 1987, it was Democrat President Bill Clinton (1993–2001) in 1996 who would proclaim 'the era of big government is over.' Both Reagan and Clinton believed that largely unregulated market forces were the best mechanism for the management and distribution of a society's resources. Players in the economy, such as banks and businesses, would always act rationally in their own self-interest. This primacy of self-interest, rather than altruism or any other non-material motive, was of course a central tenet of Randian thought. Yet it was laid bare by the financial crash of 2007–08, which resulted in government bailouts of banks and other financial institutions in many Western countries, including the USA. Yet, paradoxically, sales of Rand's books actually flourished during this time as many believed that America's impending economic collapse was brought about by too much government intervention and control. The current global Covid pandemic, at the time of writing, has brought home to many the need for huge government interventions, both in subsidizing wages during enforced lockdowns and in various 'track and trace' programmes in a bid to stop the virus spreading. What would happen in Galt's Gulch (the capitalist utopia in *Atlas Shrugged*) when a virus like Covid-19 strikes?

The American revolutionary, Patrick Henry (1736–99) urged his fellow citizens to rise up against British 'tyranny' in his famous appeal to the Virginia Convention in 1775: 'Give me liberty or give me death'. This sums up Rand's politics rather succinctly. It is perhaps no coincidence that in *Atlas Shrugged*, the hero John Galt attended the fictional Patrick Henry University.

Rand's Ideas in Practice

How might Rand's theories play out in practice, not least in a business environment? Does 'Randism', with its emphasis on self-interest rather than fairness or the impact one's actions might have on others, work in practice? An intriguing, if pessimistic, answer comes from the tale of US retail giant, Sears. In 2008, then Sears CEO, Eddie Lampert (b.1962) decided to restructure the corporation emulating Rand's economic ideas. He split the business into over 30 individual units, each with its own management and each directly accountable for its own financial results. The idea was to promote healthy and productive competition between the different units. According to Lampert, a fan of Rand and the free market, the self-interested pursuit of maximum individual profit would result in higher profits overall as each unit strove to be more productive and creative than the others. The results, however, proved otherwise. The units and their managers ended up consumed by in-fighting, becoming focused solely on their department and not the profitability of the group as a whole. As research analyst, Lynn Stuart Parramore notes:

> '*Executives started undermining other units because they knew their bonuses were tied to individual unit performance. They began to focus solely on the economic performance of their unit at the expense of the overall Sears brand. One unit, Kenmore, started selling the products of other companies and placed them more prominently than Sears' own products. Units competed for ad space in Sears' circulars, and since the unit with the most money got the most ad space, one Mother's Day circular ended up being released featuring a mini bike for boys on its cover. Units were no longer incentivized to make sacrifices, like offering discounts, to get shoppers into the store.*' (Parramore, 2013)

The value of the company roughly halved, profits fell, and thousands of workers lost their jobs. It also became a thoroughly miserable place in which to work. What the Sears example shows is that too much emphasis on the self or ego in a commercial context can lead to a complete disregard for the business as a whole, a 'get rich quick' mentality, and the opposite to the economic benefits Rand's brand of capitalism promises. Above all, perhaps, it shows how the best businesses and organizations, while driven by profits, rely on cooperation and loyalty from all levels of the workplace. In such a hypercompetitive world, many desire an escape to the sanctuary of communal support and shared interests. The unfettered free market can bring fortune to a lucky few but can also leave a string of misery and destructiveness in its path. Cooperation and competition are not necessarily the polar opposites in human nature or in economics that Rand would sometimes have us believe. It is perhaps telling that Rand was neither a businesswoman, nor a billionaire.

Conclusion

How do we measure the legacy and intellectual influence of political writers and philosophers? There is no straightforward answer, but clearly Rand has had an influence on parts of the American libertarian and Republican right, as the quote from Donald Trump and appointment of one of her supporters, Alan Greenspan, shows. Furthermore, a US Library of Congress survey found *Atlas Shrugged* coming second after the Bible in terms of influential books. Right-wing radio host Glenn Beck (b.1964) has frequently cited Rand on his shows. In popular culture, *Atlas Shrugged* makes a fleeting, albeit unflattering, appearance in the animated series 'South Park': in one episode, Officer Barbrady states that, having learnt to read and after reading *Atlas Shrugged* – which he calls garbage and something slightly cruder – he is never going to read again. *The Fountainhead* meanwhile crops up in another animated series, 'The Simpsons'. In one episode, Maggie refers to the novel as 'The Bible of right-wing losers'. Clearly then, for better or worse, Rand's writings have permeated several layers of US culture and consciousness. As Gary Weiss puts it in his study of the impact of Rand's ideas written at the time as the rise of the Tea Party movement in America, 'Yes, she was an extremist, but she matters because her extremism is no longer on the fringe.' (2013). Weiss was writing soon after Barack Obama (b.1961) had been elected as president for the first time, but the intervening years have not really altered the accuracy of his comment when it comes to the Republican right. Much of his critique of Randism sees her as the godmother of the Tea Party and a wider populist Republicanism with its vocal repudiation of statism, taxes and political correctness. Yet this impact is not just restricted to America.

There are echoes of Rand's thought in some of the sentiments of Thatcherism in the UK, even if there is no known direct link between the 'Iron Lady' and Rand (Thatcher was more influenced by the neo-liberal, Friedrich Hayek). However, there are elements of Rand's thinking in some of Thatcher's speeches, for example 'The Principles of Thatcherism' given in Korea in 1992. When describing her upbringing, Thatcher notes, 'The only life worth living, we were taught, was a life of effort'. In the same speech she argues that 'It was suggested that the collectivist approach was "inevitable", forgetting that it denies the human spirit and substitutes "state" judgment for personal responsibility.' While Thatcher was not an Objectivist and had a more traditional approach to morality and ethics than Rand, her desire to 'push back the frontiers of the state' by a major programme of privatisation, for example, puts us in mind of Rand's idea of a more minimal state. Rand's philosophy, especially regarding the seemingly unstoppable rise of the collectivist and coercive state, serves as something of a rallying cry for many on the free-market right of Western politics, though Rand is not the only voice being heard.

Unsurprisingly, then, her devotees can be found primarily in the USA, split into two main groups or factions: the Ayn Rand Institute and The Atlas Society. The former represents the original and more 'purist' approach to her writings with a focus on what Rand herself wrote and a reluctance to criticise or question her ideas, or add ideas from other later thinkers. In her biography of Rand, Anne Heller (2009) states that at the time of writing she was denied access to Rand's private papers held by the Ayn Rand Institute (ARI), though the full archives are now open to study by non-Objectivist scholars. In his study of Rand, Weiss cites an example of how the ARI expurgated an interview given by one of Rand's followers, Iris Bell, when she criticized Rand (2013). The Atlas Society is more neo-Objectivist in that, while it largely follows and embraces Rand's worldview, it does so in a broader context and is willing to embrace the ideas of other similar thinkers from neo-liberal and libertarian perspectives. The schism between the two organizations arose when David Kelley (b.1949), originally affiliated to the ARI and a friend of Peikoff, spoke at an event organized by a libertarian bookstore in 1989 and was deemed by Peikoff to have veered from the orthodox Objectivist viewpoint.

Although Rand's legacy and impact is undeniably greatest in the USA, since 2017 Rand has also become a core conservative political thinker on the A-level Politics syllabus in Britain. It is a moot point whether she would have appreciated being slotted in among political thinkers including Edmund Burke and Michael Oakeshott (1901–1990) who were very much believers in an organic view of society and the notion of duties and obligations between different social classes.

What ultimately should one make of Rand? Her proponents would say that she is a prophetic visionary with a near genius analysis of human nature. Someone more relevant than ever today, as the state gets ever larger, CCTV cameras monitor all our actions not captured by computer cookies, and human freedom shrinks in the midst of a 'cancel culture' and the dominance of special interest groups. For her critics she represents a second-rate novelist with dangerous ideas built upon shaky intellectual foundations; someone little more than another dubious American positive thinking and self-help guru, whose writings have credibility with only the ignorant and impressionable. Does she speak purely to those seeking to justify and glory in their wealth and privilege, or is she a voice of reason for those who believe in freedom and independence where many Western governments have increasingly become nanny states? Her ideas have been attacked by both sides of the political spectrum: 'The left was disgusted by her anticommunist, procapitalist policies, whereas the right was disgusted by her atheism and civil libertarianism' (Sciabarra, 1995). What is beyond doubt, is that Rand has both devotees and detractors and, whatever we might personally think of her, her work fails to leave us ambivalent.

The popularity and impact of her work has fluctuated over the years. Sales of her books and interest in her ideas tend to rise during periods when government as an institution is seen to be doomed and distrusted. This was the case for instance in the late 1960s and early 1970s, when Washington was hit by the failure of the war in Vietnam, the Watergate scandal and a stagnant economy. It was also true in the years immediately after the 2008 market crash and President Obama's election. As

Time magazine commented at the time, 'The bad economy has been good news for Rand's legacy' (Sachs, 2009).

Why does Rand leave an intellectual legacy behind at all? Not because she was a brilliant philosopher in the traditional sense, nor because her novels were literary masterpieces. Instead, what Rand offers us is a contrarian and controversial set of political ideas. It is her very extremism and binary worldview that makes objectivism a philosophy if taken in its entirety. Unsurprisingly, those who advocate such views attract ardent adherents, full of admiration for their prophet and enlightened teacher. There is even a dating service on the website, The Atlasphere, for devotees of her works. Far more numerous, though, are those for whom her ideas strike a chord and raise salient questions. How big should government be? Why shouldn't I enjoy the wealth I have? Why must I always be told to think of others first? What right has the government to regulate my actions and opinions? To all of those questions, Rand provides some interesting answers. One may well disagree with much of the overarching nature of Objectivist philosophy or see it as unrealistic in practice but, simply by reflecting on it, we are forced to face some tough questions about our own character and motives. Is human nature quite as cooperative and sharing as we like to think? Do governments and politicians always have our own best interests at heart, even in a democracy? In an increasingly secularized West, where there is less belief in the afterlife and individual liberties often appear under threat from a surveillance society, perhaps Rand's ideas still have some relevance. Like other radical political ideas such as anarchism and revolutionary communism, objectivism is something of a 'disruptor' ideology, a tool with which to analyse and critique society and human nature rather than serving as a utopian blueprint. In the preface to her biography, Heller sums Rand up succinctly and accurately: 'Gallant, driven, brilliant, brash, cruel, as accomplished as her heroes, and ultimately self-destructive, she has to be understood to be believed.' (2009)

Bibliography

Works by Rand

Rand, A. (1943) *The Fountainhead*, Penguin Books (this edition 1997)

Rand, A. (1957) *Atlas Shrugged*, Penguin Books (this edition 1997)

Rand, A. (1963) *For the New Intellectual*, Signet

Rand, A. (1964) *The Virtue of Selfishness*, New American Library

Rand, A. (1965) 'What is Capitalism' *The Objectivist Newsletter*, December 1965

Rand, A. (1966) *Capitalism: The Unknown Ideal*, New American Library

Rand, A (1969) *The Romantic Manifesto: A Philosophy of Literature*, New American Library

Rand, A. (1971) *The Return of the Primitive: The Anti-Industrial Revolution*, Penguin Group: Meridian

Rand, A. (1982) *Philosophy: Who Needs It?* Signet, New American Library, Penguin Group.

Rand, A. (1979) *The New Left: The Anti-Industrial Revolution*, New American Library

Rand, A. (1990) *Introduction to Objectivist Epistemology*, 2nd ed, New American Library

Rand, A. (2001) *The Ayn Rand Lexicon*, ed. by H. Binswanger, Penguin Books

Other works cited

Berliner, M., ed. (1995) *Letters of Ayn Rand*, New York: Dutton

Branden, N. (1984) 'The Benefits and Hazards of the Philosophy of Ayn Rand', *Journal of Humanistic Psychology*, Vol 24, Issue No 4

Brownmiller, S. (1975) *Against Our Will, Men, Women and Rape,* Simon & Schuster

Burns, J. (2011) *Goddess of the Free Market*, Oxford University Press

Butler, E. (2018) *Ayn Rand – An Introduction*, Libertarianism.org Press

Clifford, C. (2018) 'Bill and Melinda Gates: This is why we give our billions away'. *CNBC*. 13 February. Available at: https://www.cnbc.com/2018/02/13/why-bill-and-melinda-gates-give-away-billions.html [Accessed May 2022]

Daniels, A. (2010) 'Ayn Rand: engineer of souls'. *The New Criterion.* (February 2010). Appears in Vol. 40, No. 10, June 2022 edition.

Festenstein, M. and Kenney, M. (2005) *Political Ideologies*, Oxford University Press

Freedland, J. (2017) 'The new age of Ayn Rand: how she won over Trump and Silicon Valley' *The Guardian* 10 April 2017

Greenspan, A. (2007) *The Age of Turbulence: Adventures in a New World*, Penguin Press

Grossman, J.A. (2016) '5 Things To Know About Frank O'Connor, Ayn Rand's Husband', *The Atlas Society*, 9 November. Available at: https://archive.atlassociety.org/index.php/commentary/commentary-blog/6101-5-things-to-know-about-frank-o-connor-ayn-rand-s-husband. [Accessed: May 2022]

Heller, A. (2009) *Ayn Rand and the World She Made*, Anchor Books

Lossky N.O. [1917] (1928) *The World as an Organic Whole*, translated from the Russian by A. Natalie. Duddington: Oxford University Press

McConnell, S. (2010) *100 Voices: An Oral History of Ayn Rand,* Penguin Books

Marx, K. (1959) *Economic and Philosophic Manuscripts of 1844*, ed. David Riazanov, Moscow: Progress Publishers

Monypenny, W.F. and G.E. Buckle (1910) *The Life of Benjamin Disraeli: Earl of Beaconsfield*. Published by J. Murray.

Murray, A. (2010) 'Who is Ayn Rand?', *Claremont Review of Books*, Vol. X, Number 2, Spring 2010

Parramore, L. (2013) 'Ayn Rand-loving CEO destroys his empire', *Salon*, December 10, 2013

Peikoff, L. (1993) *Objectivism: The Philosophy of Ayn Rand* (Ayn Rand Library), Meridian

Powell, R. (2009) 'Embracing Power Roles Naturally: Rand's Nietzschean Heroes and Villains', *The Journal of Ayn Rand Studies*, Vol. 10, No. 2, Issue 20. pp.371–98.

Reagan, R. (1986) 'News Conference 12 August 1986', Ronald Reagan Presidential Foundation and Institute. Accessed January 2022. Available at: https://www.reaganfoundation.org/ronald-reagan/reagan-quotes-speeches/news-conference-1/

Sachs, A. (2009) 'Ayn Rand: Extremist or Visionary?' *Time Magazine*, October 2009

Sciabarra, C.M. (1995) *The Russian Radical*, Penn State Press

Smith G.H. (2016) 'Ayn Rand on Aristotle', *Libertarianism.org* (4 March, 2016). Available at: https://www.libertarianism.org/columns/ayn-rand-aristotle [Accessed: May 2022]

Vincent, A. (2010) *Modern Political Ideologies*, Wiley Blackwell

Walker, J. (1999) *The Ayn Rand Cult*, Open Court Publishing

Wallis, W. (1959) 'Ayn Rand First Interview'. Available at: https://www.youtube.com/watch?v=lHl2PqwRcY0 [Accessed May 2022]

Weiner, R. (2012) 'Paul Ryan and Ayn Rand', *The Washington Post*, 13 August, 2012. Available at: https://www.washingtonpost.com/blogs/the-fix/post/what-ayn-rand-says-about-paul-ryan/2012/08/13/fd40d574-e56d-11e1-8741-940e3f6dbf48_blog.html [Accessed May 2022]

Weiss, G. (2013) *Ayn Rand Nation*, St Martin's Press

Websites

A great deal of interesting and sometimes even balanced material about Rand is available on the Internet.

Ayn Rand Institute (ARI)

The 'official' Rand website: www.aynrand.org

Includes valuable primary sources about Rand. A contemporary cheerleader of her ideas; its approach is somewhat hagiographical and arguably glosses over some of the more dubious aspects of her life.

The Atlas Society

The 'breakaway' Rand fan club: www.atlassociety.org

Supports the broad principles of her ideas but is also open to other associated influences. As with the ARI, provides plenty of information and videos about her life and key ideas.

Libertarianism.org

Exploring the theory and history of liberty, this website contains many useful references and quotes by and about Rand.

Margaret Thatcher Foundation

www.margaretthatcher.org

A huge resource about a politician who, although not a self-declared Objectivist herself, shared many of Rand's beliefs about society and the economy.

Stanford Encyclopaedia of Philosophy

www.plato.stanford.edu/entries/ayn-rand/

Highly recommended for a more balanced summary of her ideas, and also includes an extensive bibliography.

YouTube

Unsurprisingly there are many videos about Rand on YouTube. The following interviews are highly recommended:

Ayn Rand interviewed by James Day: https://www.youtube.com/watch?v=1ixclrtypKo

Ayn Rand interviewed by Mike Wallace: https://www.youtube.com/watch?v=lHl2PqwRcY0 .

Ayn Rand interviewed by Phil Donohue: https://www.youtube.com/watch?v=WqpwTAzdPUI .

Biographics

has an excellent and balanced introduction to Rand. Available at: https://www.youtube.com/watch?v=gfE2sKfbogQ

In addition, both the ARI and The Atlas Society have uploaded videos with clear explanations of objectivism.

Biography

Simon Lemieux was born in Southampton, read Modern History at Oxford and has taught at Portsmouth Grammar School since 1988 where he is a Senior Teacher and Head of History and Politics. He has authored numerous articles for sixth form student magazines and written several politics textbooks and study guides. He is also an Assistant Editor of *Politics Review*.

Acknowledgements

I am most grateful to my good friend and colleague Dr Ruth Richmond, Head of PRS at Portsmouth Grammar School, and to Richard Fitch, for poring over an early draft of the manuscript and applying their collective insights and wisdom especially in matters philosophical. Their helpful comments and suggestions have helped ensure this book is less prone to errors of misinterpretation than would otherwise be the case. Any errors or misjudgements that remain, are my responsibility alone.

Picture Credits:

Opening Image: Ayn Rand. Photo portrait credited to "Talbot" (though not on original dust jacket). Published by the Bobbs-Merrill Company. (https://commons.wikimedia.org/wiki/File:Ayn_Rand_(1943_Talbot_portrait).jpg), „Ayn Rand (1943 Talbot portrait)", marked as public domain, more details on Wikimedia Commons: https://commons.wikimedia.org/wiki/Template:PD-US. Fig. 1 'CAPTION' Unknown author (https://commons.wikimedia.org/wiki/File:Pola_Negri_by_Ayn_Rand_cover.jpg), „Pola Negri by Ayn Rand cover", marked as public domain, more details on Wikimedia Commons: https://commons.wikimedia.org/wiki/Template:PD-Russia. Fig. 2 'CAPTION' Unknown author, possibly work for hire for Albert H. Woods, producer of the play (https://commons.wikimedia.org/wiki/File:Night_of_January_16th_jury_flyer_front.jpg), „Night of January 16th jury flyer front", marked as public domain, more details on Wikimedia Commons: https://commons.wikimedia.org/wiki/Template:PD-US. Fig. 3 'CAPTION' Photo portrait by Phyllis Cerf. Published by Random House. (https://commons.wikimedia.org/wiki/File:Ayn_Rand_(1957_Phyllis_Cerf_portrait).jpg), „Ayn Rand (1957 Phyllis Cerf portrait)", marked as public domain, more details on Wikimedia Commons: https://commons.wikimedia.org/wiki/Template:PD-US. Fig. 4 'CAPTION' Mark Paulin (https://commons.wikimedia.org/wiki/File:Ayn_Rand_Marker.jpg), „Ayn Rand Marker", marked as public domain, more details on Wikimedia Commons: https://commons.wikimedia.org/wiki/Template:PD-self. Fig. 5 'CAPTION' Works Progress Administration, Federal Art Project;, designed by Vera Bock (https://commons.wikimedia.org/wiki/File:WPA-Work-Pays-America-Poster.jpg), „WPA-Work-Pays-America-Poster", marked as public domain, more details on Wikimedia Commons: https://commons.wikimedia.org/wiki/Template:PD-US. Fig. 6 'CAPTION' Published by Random House. Jacket design by George Salter. (https://commons.wikimedia.org/wiki/File:Atlas_Shrugged_(1957_1st_ed)_-_Ayn_Rand.jpg), „Atlas Shrugged (1957 1st

Who the hell is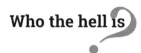

This exciting new series of books sets out to explore the life and theories of the world's leading intellectuals in a clear and understandable way. The series currently includes the following subject areas:

Art History | Psychology | Philosophy | Sociology | Politics

For more information about forthcoming titles in the Who the hell is...? series, go to: **www.whothehellis.co.uk**.

If any of our readers would like to put in a request for a particular intellectual to be included in our series, then please contact us at **info@whothehellis.co.uk**.